Parenting is serious business. We live in a crazy, messed-up world—especially when it comes to marriage, dating, sex, and family. Satan and the demons have kicked their attacks on God's institution of the family into high gear. Is there anything we can do to help our children reject the lies of the world and prepare themselves to follow God's plan for manhood, womanhood, marriage, and the family? That is what *Preparing Children for Marriage* is all about. Let me warn you: this book is not for the faint of heart. It is real, honest, candid, and courageous. It will make you think, rattle your cage, drive you to have needed conversations with your kids, and, most importantly, cause you to dig into the Bible for a practical plan to help your children love and follow Jesus.

    —Rob Rienow, Founder, Visionary Family Ministries

Josh Mulvihill has done a great job of explaining dating and what a Christian marriage should look like. Parents will find thought-provoking guidance to use with their children when discussing dating, sexual issues, and marriage. Divorced parents struggle to find ways to teach their children what a God-designed marriage looks like, but this book lays it out very clearly. It will also open readers' eyes to the sinful challenges our children are currently facing regarding sexual issues and what is being taught in many schools today.

    —Linda Jacobs, Founder, DivorceCare for Kids

Preparing Children for Marriage will equip you to sharpen your thinking, increase your impact, and influence young people to apply the truth of God's Word to their lives. This book is biblical and practical and is a valuable tool for parents and grandparents.

    —Kevin Leman, Author, *Have a New Kid by Friday* and *The Birth Order Book*

This eye-opening book shows what is missing and what is needed in order for our children to have a biblical view of marriage. With insight, Josh Mulvihill shows parents and ministry leaders how to proactively seize developmental milestones in order to help prepare the next generation to embrace and uphold God-honoring marriages and be bright, shining stars in a very dark world.

> —**Pat Cimo**, Director of Marriage and Family Life, Willow Creek Community Church, South Barrington, Illinois

Josh Mulvihill has written a thought-provoking book to help parents prepare their children for marriage. As a pastor, Josh delivers insight and experience in addition to unpacking God's truth in creative ways. His "courageous conversations," or talks parents should have with their children, are worth the price of the book alone. For parents and those working with children, Josh's book will be an excellent resource as we prepare the next generation for lifelong marriage.

> —**Ken Canfield**, Founder, National Center for Fathering

Preparing Children for Marriage is a lifeline in a sea of sexual and marital confusion. Every parent, pastor, and educator who is serious about helping the children in his or her care to develop a biblical worldview should read and use this book.

> —**Jeff Keaton**, Founder and President, Renewanation

By default our kids get plenty of sex education these days, and most of it is not only wrong but very harmful. Josh Mulvihill has given us the antidote: a beautifully written and very practical guide for parents who want to make sure their children have a strong biblical foundation not only for making wise choices but for building healthy marriages. I urge all Christian parents not only to read this book but to put it into practice right away!

> —**Wayne Rice**, Cofounder, Youth Specialties; Director of Conferencing, The Legacy Coalition; Author, *Generation to Generation*

In a day when young people invest the greater part of their time in their wedding event itself, they need more time to prepare for marriage.

Parents can powerfully engage their kids with the topics that will set them up for success in their marriages, the way God intended.

Waiting until marital counseling is too late—this book needs to be in the hands of every parent with children!

—**Ron Hunter Jr.**, Director, D6 Conference; Author, *The DNA of D6*

Parents, if you're wondering how to talk to your kids about sex, you will not find a better resource than this book. Josh Mulvihill's approach is straight from the Bible, full of great insight and advice, and incredibly helpful. If you think it's not time for "the talk" yet, better think again—Josh's argument for a childhood-long approach to teaching your child about sex and marriage will change your mind and at the same time equip you for many talks. You will want to read this book and then put it somewhere handy so you can refer to it again and again.

—**Larry Fowler**, Founder, The Legacy Coalition

In *Preparing Children for Marriage*, Josh Mulvihill has given parents an invaluable resource to help them present a biblical worldview of sexuality, marriage, and dating to their children. This book is practical, biblical, and chock-full of great discussion-starting questions. *Someone* is going to shape your children's views on these topics—so take my advice, get this book, and allow Josh to help you be the one to disciple your children in these critical areas.

—**Marty Machowski**, Family Life Pastor, Covenant Fellowship Church, Glen Mills, Pennsylvania; Author, *The Ology*

Wow! What a great book to empower parents to have early-and-often discussions with their children about love, sex, and marriage. Josh Mulvihill has created a biblical tool that parents can use to help their kids challenge the worldly version of "normal" that they are exposed to regularly. I will commend this book to all parents and encourage them to use the Courageous Conversation sections at the end of each chapter to engage their kids in specific conversations in order to embed convictions in their hearts.

—**Scott Turansky**, Cofounder, National Center for Biblical Parenting

PREPARING
CHILDREN
FOR
MARRIAGE

PREPARING
CHILDREN
FOR
MARRIAGE

How to Teach God's Good Design
for Marriage, Sex, Purity, and Dating

JOSH MULVIHILL

P&R
P U B L I S H I N G
P.O. BOX 817 • PHILLIPSBURG • NEW JERSEY 08865-0817

Library of Congress Cataloging-in-Publication Data

Names: Mulvihill, Josh, author.
Title: Preparing children for marriage : how to teach God's good design for marriage, sex, purity, and dating / Josh Mulvihill.
Description: Phillipsburg : P&R Publishing, 2017.
Identifiers: LCCN 2017026454| ISBN 9781629951805 (pbk.) | ISBN 9781629951812 (epub) | ISBN 9781629951829 (mobi)
Subjects: LCSH: Parenting--Religious aspects--Christianity. | Child rearing--Religious aspects--Christianity. | Marriage—Religious aspects--Christianity. | Sex--Religious aspects--Christianity. | Dating (Social customs)--Religious aspects--Christianity.
Classification: LCC BV4529 .M85 2017 | DDC 248.8/45--dc23
LC record available at https://lccn.loc.gov/2017026454

To Jay, Asher, Kate, Jon, and Emily.

Remember four things:

Marry only in Christ.
Pursue holiness, and happiness will follow.
Marriage is the joining of two sinners, not two saints.
You are loved.

If you were going to live in a foreign country, would you prepare?
If you were going to become an astronaut, would you prepare?
If you were going to become a concert pianist, would you prepare?
And so how do your sons prepare for the mystery of marriage? . . .
Are they just making time until it "happens" to them?
—*Douglas Wilson,* Future Men

◆ ◆ ◆

Happy are the marriages which observe three rules:
1. Marry only in the Lord and only after God's approval and blessing.
2. Do not expect too much from your spouse, remembering that
marriage is the union of two sinners, not two angels.
3. Strive for one's growth in Christ. The more holy people are,
the more happier they are.
—*J. C. Ryle,* Expository Thoughts on the Gospels

CONTENTS

Foreword by Tedd Tripp   11

Acknowledgments   13

Introduction   15

Overview of the Book   19

Part 1: Getting Started

1. Don't Be a Conversation Short   25
   Raising Your Child in a Sex-Saturated Culture

2. When and How Do You Begin?   37
   Starting Early with Scripture

3. How to Communicate with Your Child   47
   The ABCs of Talking about Marriage, Dating, and Sex

Part 2: Marriage

4. An Overview of Marriage   61
   Five Truths Every Child Must Know

5. What Is Marriage? (Part 1)   71
   Marriage Is for One Man and One Woman

6. What Is Marriage? (Part 2)   79
   Marriage Is a Lifelong Covenant

7. Why Did God Create Marriage?   91
   Three of God's Good Purposes for Marriage

9

CONTENTS

8. Preparing Your Son for Marriage   103
   Embracing His Role as Husband

9. Preparing Your Daughter for Marriage   119
   Embracing Her Role as Wife

10. Preparing Your Child for Singleness   135
    Finding Satisfaction in God Rather Than Marriage

Part 3: Sex and Purity

11. What Biblical Truths Does Your Child Need to Know
    about Sex?   145
    Remembering God's Good Plan and Purpose

12. How to Have "the Talk"   157
    Using Proverbs 5

13. Preparing Your Child for Purity   167
    Three Biblical Methods to Implement

14. Talking to Your Child about Pornography and Lust   181
    Three Ways to Help Your Child Strive for Holiness

15. Are Crushes Okay?   191
    Responding to Attraction in a Way That Honors God

Part 4: Dating

16. What Is the Purpose of Dating?   199
    Dating Is a Method—with a Goal

17. Dating and Parents   207
    Being a Wise Ally to Your Child

18. Whom Should Your Child Date?   219
    Following Biblical Guidelines

Conclusion: Final Thoughts   237
Appendix A: A Word to Grandparents   239
Appendix B: The Wisdom of Faithfulness (Proverbs 5)   245

FOREWORD

"Okay, kids, we're going to Auntie's house. You should take a good book along, because you know she doesn't have any toys for you to play with. Amusing yourselves quietly is one of the ways we can show love and respect for Auntie."

Good parents are always preparing their kids for what comes next. We do this in both great and small ways. We prepare them for a new brother or sister. We talk through new expectations as their educational journeys unfold. We prepare them for driving or for their first job. Whether in the little things like a visit with a maiden aunt or the big things like going off to college, parents are always getting their children ready for what comes next.

No transition has greater significance than marriage does. The Bible captures the magnitude of this transition in the statement "Therefore a man shall leave his father and his mother and hold fast to his wife, and they shall become one flesh" (Gen. 2:24). There is no way to overstate the importance of helping our children to find their life partner and prepare to leave home in order to establish a new family.

In his role as a pastor and discipler of children and young people, Josh Mulvihill has thought deeply about marriage and the biblical truths one must understand and embrace before embarking on it. He has developed this comprehensive guide that will equip you to help your kids get ready for the joys and challenges of a one-flesh relationship.

Mulvihill understands a fundamental truth that many parents miss: Parents must provide their children with a fully populated Christian culture of understanding if the callings of Christian living are to make sense. Simply telling them what to expect and what to do is not enough. One has to work out the implications—not only of our callings, but of the foundational truths that make sense of those callings.

What *Preparing Children for Marriage* provides is a comprehensive picture of marriage. Who is marriage for? How does it work? Why did God create marriage? How does one prepare a son or a daughter for marriage? What does the Bible teach about sexuality and moral purity? How can we help kids avoid the temptations that potentially damage marriage? How do the differing roles of men and women in marriage change what a boy or a girl must understand? These and many related topics make this a comprehensive paradigm of what our children must know in order to be prepared for marriage. There is even a section on preparing our children for singleness, if that is God's plan for them.

While there is nothing here that breaks new ground theologically, the value of *Preparing Children for Marriage* is hard to overstate, for at least three reasons. (1) Josh Mulvihill has thought more comprehensively than most of us about these issues. (2) He has organized his study into helpful conversational topics (at the end of each chapter you will find a valuable guide to conversations with your children). (3) He reminds us that getting our kids ready for marriage is not something that we do in the months before they take that big step. Preparing them for marriage is a life-long proposition.

I have three adult children. I have always been fairly self-conscious about childrearing issues, and I would have benefitted from this book. I am sure you will as well. I look forward to giving it to my children so they will be equipped to prepare their children for marriage.

Tedd Tripp
August 2017

ACKNOWLEDGMENTS

Preparing Children for Marriage has been a decade-long project that began when Leah King asked a middle school pastor, who had only a toddler of his own, to have "the talk" with her teenage son. Little did I know that request would eventually lead to this book. Thank you, Leah, for blessing me with the opportunity to speak into your son's life. It was a joy to work with you on the early stages of this project and to create a small booklet to equip parents for the gigantic task of teaching God's truth to their children.

Amanda Martin, thank you for your steady and diligent editing efforts. Your high standards were both a blessing and a curse, but I trust that the finished product will honor God and help many young people. Thank you for your patience in working with a new author and for your dedication to seeing a text that is faithful to Scripture and fruitful for families. You are an excellent editor and have made me a better author.

Dad, thanks for intentionally teaching me the truth of God's Word as it relates to marriage and for being the kind of parent this book describes. Your intentionality, consistency, and faithfulness are gifts that continue to keep giving. Many of the things I encourage parents to do in this book were learned from you. Thanks for the informal conversations, gentle guidance, needed correction, and enforced boundaries. And I'll even say thank you for drawing a diagram of fallopian tubes in the snow when we were squirrel hunting. I hope I can train my own children as well as you trained yours.

My dearest Jen, I could not ask for a better wife. Your grace, godliness, gentleness, and wisdom are gifts to so many people. I am delighted that our children have an Ephesians 5 and Proverbs 31 woman to look to and learn from. What a joy it is to see you pointing our children to the cross and calling them to live a life that matters for Christ. Thanks for helping to write the courageous conversation questions, for your editing advice, and for having the patience to see this project to the end. If our sons married women who were anything like you, it would be a true blessing.

And lastly, thank you P&R Publishing for believing in the message of this book and taking a chance on a new author. I have been blessed by the ministry heart that drives the decisions at P&R and am happy to have my name associated with such a wonderful organization.

Introduction

In all my years as a pastor, I've found that few topics generate more interest or angst than dating and marriage. Parents regularly contact me for guidance and resources to help them prepare their children for this critical time of life.

Many years ago, a number of single mothers approached me and asked me to take their sons away for a weekend to have "the talk." I agreed and began the task of finding resources to help equip these young boys for marriage. What I found was a lot of resources about purity and puberty. I found books that taught young people to remain sexually pure and to expect physical changes in adolescence, but I couldn't find a resource that taught young people the biblical principles of marriage.

If you search the market, you will find plenty of books about marriage for adults, but you will have a difficult time finding a book that helps parents teach the biblical truths of marriage to their children. In addition, you can find very good books on dating and purity, but you won't find all these topics in the same book.

Parents already have the most valuable tool for preparing their children for marriage. The Bible is sufficient for all matters of life and godliness (see 2 Peter 1:3), but few parents use it to address this subject. Most overlook it. Few know how to apply it to preparing their children for marriage. Many look to sources outside Scripture for dealing with this subject, using the Bible as a seasoning. Yet the Bible contains the foundational truths parents need in order to successfully train children for marriage, dating, and purity. If children know the basic foundational truths of Scripture, they can apply those truths in any and every scenario that confronts them.

While I can't touch on every subject related to marriage, dating, and purity in this book, I have four main goals:

- to see young people treasure Christ and live in a God-honoring way
- to equip parents, grandparents, pastors, and Christian educators to teach the biblical principles of marriage to children, and at the earliest possible age
- to provide a one-stop shop on these topics for young people of all ages
- to generate discussion that will drive parents and their children to God's Word

Are You Prepared?

The Bible teaches that God created marriage for his glory and man's good and that marriage is the expected norm for men and women. God has placed within us the desire to love and to be loved. This desire is good and should be pursued in its proper time. It may be strange for a young person to think of himself or herself as a future married person; however, it is also one of the most profitable thoughts that young people can have.

This is a foundation-laying book that will provide theological training for a critical area of parenting. I will provide a biblical definition for marriage and will explore the primary passages that can be used to train children in this area. If you are unclear about the meaning and purpose of marriage, you cannot provide the proper guidance to young people or effectively prepare them for a marriage that pleases God.

Too often, the church addresses these topics with young people and does not include the parents in any significant way. This robs parents of an opportunity to nurture their children's faith and minimizes children's interactions with their parents during an important milestone of life. It is my desire to see parents and grandparents taking an active role in the preparation of children for marriage, and this book is a tool for that purpose.

While it is the role of parents to train their children, their discussions of marriage in the home do not negate the need for discussions in the church as well. The church has an important role to play itself in the preparation of children for marriage. God has given the church the mission of discipling all its members and teaching them the full counsel of God. Churches cannot neglect teaching this topic to children, but they do need to be discerning in how they address it, and this book will provide some direction.

Churches and families must work together in presenting a unified message because society makes it exceedingly difficult to be holy. Culture communicates powerful messages about dating and marriage, and young people without strong, consistent biblical teaching and parental example are likely to be influenced toward unbiblical views. Homosexuality and divorce are inconsistent with God's plan for marriage, yet young people are confronted with the argument that marriage between one man and one woman for an entire lifetime is outdated and closed-minded.

Young people are also in danger of making marriage into a me-focused, romance-intoxicated, Christ-neglecting "thing." We must protect against and root out this culturally contaminated view by teaching the truth of Scripture to our children. It is my prayer that your child embraces an eternal, high, Christ-glorifying view of marriage. The days of "first comes love, then comes marriage, then comes baby in the baby carriage" are long gone in American culture. Even Christian children are getting the order wrong. It is critical that parents teach a correct biblical order to love, marriage, and sex through words and actions. Chances are, your children are not hearing this anywhere else.

Preparation for marriage can begin today as you teach your child biblical principles about marriage, pray for your child's future spouse, and help your child protect his or her heart from sexual immorality. Knowing what God desires for a young person will help that young person to prepare for one of the most important decisions of his or her life.

OVERVIEW OF THE BOOK

The lessons in this book should prove helpful for children of all ages, from early elementary through high school, and can be used by parents, grandparents, pastors, small groups, Sunday school classes, health curriculums, and college classes. Anyone who has a spiritual influence in the life of a child can use this book to teach that child the truths of God's Word and point him or her to Christ.

Children's grade school years are the ideal time to begin in-depth discussions with them about marriage, dating, and purity. Biologically, children will be interested in members of the opposite sex when they are around nine or ten years old. Preemptively addressing this subject allows parents to be the first and loudest voice that their children will hear on it. Paul David Tripp refers to the preteen years as "the age of opportunity"[1] and encourages parents to intentionally utilize this time of life. Parents have a window, prior to the teenage years, when children are open and receptive to parental guidance. Wise parents capitalize on this opportunity and reinforce the same truths as children age.

Parents are often unaware of the need to address this topic early. I continually hear from parents about sexual experiences their children have had much sooner than the parents anticipated. A high

1. Paul David Tripp, *Age of Opportunity: A Biblical Guide to Parenting Teens*, 2nd ed. (Phillipsburg, NJ: P&R Publishing, 2001).

percentage of parents expect that the middle and high school years will be filled with dating and purity challenges, but many do not realize that this happens for many students as early as kindergarten. This book will help parents teach the truths of God's Word to a young child and a teenager in an age-appropriate and comprehensive way.

A Note to Church Leaders

If you are a pastor (or a children's or youth director) and you work with young people, I want to point out that you have a responsibility to address these topics with children as well. Moses, Joshua, Nehemiah, and Paul all taught children about marriage and sex. However, in each instance, parents were always present. I have taught on these topics many times, on Wednesday nights and Sunday mornings, with young people ranging from kindergarten through twelfth grade. I have found that three things make this a success.

Communicating Plans to Parents in Advance

I do this by email a few weeks before tackling the topic. If anything, you should overcommunicate. Surprising parents with this topic is not a good idea. You want to avoid a scenario in which parents learn what their child was taught on the car ride home.

Including a Word-for-Word Manuscript of the Talk

This eliminates fear and builds trust with parents. If you are interested in what this looks like, appendix B is one of the lessons that I teach kindergartners through sixth graders on marriage. I send this as an attachment to parents.

Inviting Parents to Join You

Many parents will learn along with their children. One of my most memorable moments came when I invited parents of fifth and sixth graders to join me as I taught through Genesis 2 and the meaning of marriage. A room that seated almost three hundred was filled to capacity, and about a half dozen parents brought video cameras and tripods to record the teaching. I invite parents because I want to honor them as the primary spiritual influence in their children's lives, but I also teach on the subject in order to be faithful to God and the responsibility he has given me as a pastor.

Part 1: Getting Started

Parents often ask, "What subjects should I address with my child, and at what age?" and "When is it appropriate to talk to children about marriage, sex, and dating?" To answer these questions, I explore the pattern of what the Bible teaches to young people at what ages, and I encourage you to follow God's example. I also provide communication guidelines in order to help you avoid major land mines and create fruitful discussion as you navigate the rest of the topics in this book with your child.

Once children understand biblical principles and are given applications of them, they can apply Scripture as their life situations demand. One of our jobs as parents is to teach the biblical principles that children need to know and help children make wise, God-honoring decisions as opportunities arise.

Part 2: Marriage

Part 2 focuses on teaching children the biblical principles of marriage. Young people will learn what marriage is, what it is not, and why God created it. This section will also equip parents to prepare their children for the roles of husband and wife. Each chapter ends with a series of Bible study questions for generating discussion.

Part 3: Sex and Purity

Part 3 demonstrates how to teach a child about sex from a biblical perspective and teaches parents how to have "the talk" with their children using Proverbs 5. The section also addresses how a young person can remain sexually pure in a hypersexual culture.

Part 4: Dating

In this last section, I help parents and children to think about dating in a biblical and balanced way, answering the following questions: What's the purpose of dating? How old should a person be in order to date? What is a parent's role in a child's dating life? What kind of person should you date? And what are the biblical criteria for choosing a spouse?

Many adults have regrets about the dating decisions they made themselves while in middle or high school. Your children have the opportunity to avoid this fate and to look back on their dating days with fondness because their actions were pleasing to God, to you, and to their future spouses. Most importantly, your child has the opportunity to choose a spouse who loves Jesus and to display the gospel through his or her marriage.

◆◆◆ PART 1 ◆◆◆

GETTING STARTED

1

Don't Be a Conversation Short

Raising Your Child in a Sex-Saturated Culture

"Help!" the parent of a sixth grader said to me. "Last night my son was video chatting with a female classmate of his and was exposed to something he shouldn't have been." The sadness in her words told me that something unfortunate was coming.

"Someone joked that she should flash him. He didn't expect that she actually would. He feels so bad about what happened that he threw up this morning."

The parents of this sixth-grade child are good parents. They long to be faithful to Scripture and are passionate to see their son grow up to love the Lord. Both mom and dad had engaged spiritually in their son's life and taken specific, proactive steps to protect his purity and prepare him for the challenges he would face. Unfortunately, it had not occurred to them that a sixth-grade girl might bare herself live on a video call.

"I knew things like this could eventually be an issue," the mother continued, "but I didn't expect them until high school. I also thought we had prepared for this, but I found that we were one conversation short."

One conversation short. That is an unfortunate statement when it comes to issues that affect our children as much as marriage, dating, and purity. There isn't a single parent who aims to be one conversation short, yet many well-intentioned parents find themselves in this same unexpected place.

Many young Christians are not adequately prepared to handle the sexual tidal wave and the unbiblical views of marriage that are presented to them, and often they are left to discern for themselves whether what they hear is true. To compound the problem, children are confronted at a formative age by adults with well-thought-out arguments that sound plausible. The combination can be lethal for children who are naturally trusting, are unsure of the Bible's teachings, and lack a strong parental voice that is speaking God's truth at home.

Children are met with unbiblical views of sex and marriage through the Internet, in the media, in education, from peers, and even by some trusted religious leaders or family members. Take a moment to explore with me what our children are being exposed to and at what age. It is critical that you know the messages that are being communicated so you can counter those messages with the life-giving truth of God's Word.

Although many examples could be chosen, I will introduce you to two books and one organization that embody the essence of the unbiblical teaching that confronts children today. All children, including yours, will have to contend with these ideas at some point. The fact that these messages are being communicated necessitates a proactive posture from every parent.

Two Books

King and King, a picture book by Linda de Haan and Stern Nijland, is read in many public school classrooms around the country. Written for children as young as kindergarten, it follows a familiar story line—that of a queen finding her king—except with a twist: two men fall in love and get married. The pictures in the book are descriptive and present the two men as happy and their marriage as normal. There are pictures of the men holding hands, participating in a wedding ceremony, and kissing. No overt arguments are made; a story is simply told. It is a powerful way to teach young children an unbiblical view of marriage.

Another potent picture book, *My Princess Boy*, tells the story of a young boy who wants to wear a dress to school but fears being made fun of by his classmates. Cheryl Kilodavis, the boy's mother, wrote the book to convince young children to accept, and not question, people who want to dress and act like those of the opposite gender. Children are encouraged to view cross-dressing transgender individuals as no different from others, suggesting that gender confusion is normal. As Christians, we do not want our children to tease or bully anyone but to love them unconditionally as God has loved us. However, this story-book seeks to normalize transgenderism and can lead to gender confusion by suggesting that it is acceptable to reject our God-given gender.

By introducing you to these two books, I want to show you first-hand how our children are being taught an unbiblical view of marriage, purity, and sex. Ideas are introduced when children are young, then reinforced through different avenues as children age. Parents are often unaware that this is happening. From the child's point of view, he or she is being read a picture book just like Mom or Dad would read before bed. It seems harmless. But subtle, dangerous, unbiblical world views are being taught, and parents must know about them and be proactive.

As you'll see, *King and King* and *My Princess Boy* are just the tip of the iceberg.

Meet SIECUS

I want to introduce you to the Sexuality Information and Education Council of the United States (SIECUS). More than likely you have never heard of this organization, but, if you have a child in the public school system, you are being impacted by its curriculum. For over a decade, SIECUS has published *Guidelines for Comprehensive Sexuality Education: Kindergarten–12th Grade* to help educators teach a robust sex education curriculum. SIECUS claims that "the *Guidelines* have become one of the most influential publications in the field and a trusted resource for educators, curriculum developers, and school administrators."[1] It goes on to say, "It is our sincere hope . . . to ensure that all young people receive the comprehensive education about sexuality they need to become sexually healthy adults."[2]

The words "sexually healthy adults" should catch your attention. What is a sexually healthy adult? According to whose standards? And on what authority? You'll soon see that a sexually healthy adult defined by SIECUS looks very different from the sexually healthy adult who follows God's teaching in the Bible. SIECUS encourages children to seek pleasure, explore desire, reject external ethics, and decide for themselves what is right.

Although SIECUS states that parents should be a child's primary sex educator, it either assumes that parents are not teaching children on this topic or believes that trained professionals can do a better job. Certainly a percentage of parents are failing to train and prepare their children, but I have found that Christian parents are very concerned about this topic, know it is their job to prepare their children for marriage, and desire to be effective in this area of parenting. In most instances, it is far more effective to work with a parent than to try to work around a parent. SIECUS's school-based sex education is meant to replace parents' teaching at every grade level.

Although I'll provide a brief overview of the *Guidelines* here, I encourage you to look up this sex education material online (see footnote 1) so that you can see for yourself what concepts children are exposed to in American culture. Here is a brief summary.

Marriage and divorce. SIECUS defines marriage as a legal agreement between the married couple and the government[3] and teaches

---

1. National Guidelines Task Force, *Guidelines for Comprehensive Sexuality Education: Kindergarten–12th Grade*, 3rd ed. (Washington, D.C.: Sexuality Information and Education Council of the United States, 2004), 5, available online at http://www.siecus.org/_data/global/images/guidelines.pdf.
2. Ibid.
3. See ibid., 39.

children that there is no real difference in commitment between married and cohabiting couples.[4] Divorce is simply what happens when people decide to split up.[5] This is very different from the Bible's description of marriage as a lifelong covenant made by a man and woman before God (we'll explore this more in part 2).

Gender roles. Starting in kindergarten, SIECUS wants to discredit the idea that "boys and girls behave in certain [gender specific] ways."[6] By middle school, students are being told, "Individuals should be allowed to make their own choices about appropriate roles for themselves as men and women."[7] As for gender identity, this comes from a person's "internal sense" of whether they are male, female, or a mix of both.[8] We'll look at God's good design for men and women in chapters 8 and 9.

Homosexuality. SIECUS instructs children about homosexuality from the very beginning, teaches that "people of all sexual orientations can have relationships that are equally fulfilling,"[9] and wants children to believe that some of them are homosexual and "can be attracted to and fall in love with someone of the same gender."[10] It also normalizes two-dad and two-mom families.[11]

Masturbation. Children as young as kindergarten are introduced to the idea of "touching and rubbing one's own genitals to feel good."[12] Later they learn that "many" young people masturbate.[13]

4. See ibid.
5. See ibid.
6. Ibid., 72.
7. Ibid.
8. Ibid., 31.
9. Ibid., 29.
10. Ibid.
11. See ibid., 34.
12. Ibid., 51.
13. Ibid., 52.

Pornography. In high school, students are told that "some people" use pornography to "enhance their sexual fantasies."[14] Rather than flee from sexual urges, grade-school-aged children are encouraged to embrace sexual feelings and fantasies and are told that sexual desires are natural.[15]

Sexual activity. Middle schoolers learn that they can "give and receive sexual pleasure" in "many ways," even without sexual intercourse.[16] In high school, young people are taught that "many teenagers have had sexual intercourse and many have not."[17]

Avoiding parental oversight. Young people are pointed in the direction of organizations and websites[18] where they can discuss homosexuality without their parents' knowledge. Middle schoolers are told that "some agencies . . . provide services for teenagers that do not require parental permission, are confidential, and cost little or no money."[19] Seventh and eighth graders are also told that, depending on their state, they may not need parental permission to be prescribed contraception.[20]

These guidelines should trouble Christians at every age level. First, they contradict the Bible and often teach the opposite of what God instructs in his Word. Children are being taught an erroneous definition of marriage, a faulty understanding of who may marry whom, and an unbiblical view of the roles of men and women in marriage. Children are encouraged to explore sexual desires at very young ages and are given damaging guidance about gender identity, abortion, homosexuality, cohabitation, and divorce.

14. Ibid., 56.
15. See ibid., 51.
16. Ibid., 54.
17. Ibid.
18. See ibid., 30.
19. Ibid., 49.
20. See ibid., 59.

Second, these guidelines encourage certain behaviors and plant ideas in children's minds, suggesting that the behaviors are normal and good. The statements are subtle, but many of them equate to an immoral how-to manual. They imply that young people can and should use porn, touch themselves for pleasure, take emergency contraception, and contact organizations to talk about homosexuality without their parents' knowledge. These are presented as "options" or "ideas," but they are more than that. Why would you give children options that you don't want them to act on?

The Missionary Zeal of Our Sexual Culture

The culture we live in celebrates sexual sin by making it readily available to anyone, at any time, in any location. We should be diligent to shield our children from as much evil as possible for as long as possible. But there will come a day in every child's life when he or she is exposed to sexual sin or unbiblical teaching about sex and marriage. For most children, such as the boy in my opening story, this happens sooner rather than later. In my experience, major exposure of some form happens to most children by their early to mid elementary years. Barrett Johnson has made similar observations.

> I used to say that parents need to "get these issues on the table," but the reality is that they are already on the table. Our kids are being exposed to a constant stream of messages from their friends and the media and the world about relationships and sex. Most of these messages are far from the truth. Okay, let me be blunt: they are outright lies. These lies have the power to create in our kids a worldview that will impact their sexuality and their marriages for the rest of their lives. . . .
>
> Current research, common sense, and the Biblical directive all scream this one truth: parents have significant power and influence over this dimension of their kids' lives. Moms and dads must enter into the discussion early and start defining

some truths before the world begins to overwhelm their kids with lies.[21]

Due to our culture, children are exposed to a lot of sexual content. They receive a robust, secular sex education and are taught society's views about marriage. As a result, many children are absorbing a secular, self-indulgent, antibiblical worldview. At best, many young people are confused about what is good, right, true, and noble related to marriage, dating, and purity. At worst, they are being set on a trajectory away from Christ.

Much is at stake. These are life-altering, eternity-impacting, major worldview issues.[22] The health of your child's soul, marriage, walk with Jesus, and trajectory in life depend in part on what he or she believes and how he or she behaves when it comes to purity, dating, and marriage. Parents who spend most of their time talking about the body's biological functions and changes in puberty are addressing helpful subjects but are missing the most important topics.

The missionary zeal of our sexual culture is operating in full force. Young people hear messages such as "My body, my choice" and "If it feels so good, how can it be so wrong?" Parents must counter these cultural messages with the truth of God's Word or cultural confusion will seep into our children's hearts just as it did into the Corinthian church (see 1 Cor. 6:12–20).

Some people in the Corinthian church believed that religious prostitution benefitted the spiritual life and aided a person's relationship with God. Some believed that having sex was as natural and necessary as eating food. The church at Corinth had embraced the cultural belief that "everything is permissible" and used this to justify their actions (see 1 Cor. 6:12). They dismissed the importance of sexual purity due to the faulty belief that God would destroy the

21. Barrett Johnson, *The Talks: A Parent's Guide to Critical Conversations about Sex, Dating, and Other Unmentionables* (Atlanta: INFO for Families, 2014), 12.

22. For an explanation of the worldview behind the sexual revolution, see Nancy Pearcey, *Total Truth: Liberating Christianity from its Cultural Captivity* (Wheaton, IL: Crossway, 2005), 142–46.

body, and so it didn't matter what they did with their bodies. Paul responded that, just because something is biologically possible, this does not make it morally permissible. His guiding principle is that our bodies belong to God and are to be used in a way that honors him.

The state of the church at Corinth sends a loud warning to parents today. That group of Scripture-loving, Christ-following people had their sexual practices all wrong. They couldn't differentiate what was right from wrong. They looked more like the city of Corinth than the people of Christ. What occurred at the church of Corinth can easily happen in the hearts of our children. Richard Pratt's comments on 1 Corinthians 6 are worth considering: "Christians are easily influenced by the standards of the world. When we grow up in a culture that tells us certain practices are good, we tend to embrace these practices even as we follow Christ. Every Christian has such cultural blind spots."[23]

Plenty of children—and possibly your own—are in danger of embracing our culture's powerful messages, even as they seek to follow Christ. Perhaps some of the SIECUS guidelines didn't seem alarming to you. It is challenging to recognize a cultural blind spot. Worldly influence in the hearts of our children is hard to detect, because it takes time for weeds to grow. With God's grace and proper training, our children can be Bible-believing Christians who are spiritual salmon, swimming against the current of culture.

Parents have the critical job of articulating and embodying a biblical vision of marriage to their children. Unless our children are well grounded in Scripture, they will look more like culture than like Christ. Our children need the soul-gripping, life-shaping words of Scripture to ground them, to guide them, and to guard them.

Take a moment and think about your child. When your child encounters a message about sex or marriage, such as the topics from SIECUS, is he or she able to test what is said against the Bible? Would he or she be swayed into believing and acting on the message being

---

23. Richard L. Pratt Jr., *1 & 2 Corinthians*, Holman New Testament Commentary (Nashville: B&H Publishing, 2000), 97.

taught, or would your child be able to spot the error and stand firm in his or her faith?

An Encouraging Note

While there is much for us to be alarmed about, it is sinful for the Christian to live in a state of worry and fear. We instruct our children because we are motivated by love and want what is best for them, not because we are frightened.

God is the God of hope who is sovereignly in control over all. Parents can rest in the God of refuge and turn to him for joy, strength, and peace. Enemies will attack our children's hearts, but this knowledge should not debilitate or discourage us. Instead, it should motivate us to action and remind us that there is a battle raging for our children's hearts. Parents and grandparents must intentionally live out Deuteronomy 6:4–9 and diligently train their children to know the truth and love the Lord.

The following email illustrates parents who are doing just that. It is my hope that you will be encouraged by this story and be given a vision, even if only a small one, for the role you must play in your child's life when it comes to the topics of dating, marriage, and sex.

Just wanted to share with you a cool conversation my daughter had with her close group of friends from school. There are four of them who have been hanging out together since sixth grade, one of whom has been a good friend since first grade. Anyway, she had a sleepover with them on Friday night, and at some point the conversation turned to prom night (a few years off yet, thankfully). Two of the girls said that they fully expected to rent a hotel room after prom and have sex, because it was expected and "everyone" does it. My daughter stood up to them and told them she wasn't planning on "doing it" because she wants to wait until her wedding night. Then she explained about the purity ring she was wearing and what it stood for. She said there was absolute silence in the room for at least thirty seconds while they thought about it. Then someone asked, "What if the guy you date expects it? What will you do then?" To which she responded, "I plan on dating a guy who holds to the same values and morals that I do so that it won't be an issue." She was so excited because she had prayed, before going over there, that she would be a good witness for Christ. At some point she hopes to bring God into the conversation as to why she has the morals she does. I encouraged her to do so and said I was proud of her for stating what she believed. I think God will honor that step of faith.

Praise the Lord for parents who have prepared their children for this type of experience and have done so using biblical principles and proven methods. The purity ring was evidence that these parents took their role seriously, and it it obvious that what they taught their daughter made an impact. What if these parents had not taught their child God's truth about marriage? What path might she have gone down later in life as a result of being influenced by her friends' decisions?

There is an important point to be made here. Many of the decisions our children make today are a result of convictions they have formed months or even years beforehand. The manifestation of those convictions, or lack thereof, typically takes time to fully bear fruit. This is why it is critical that biblical truths are taught early in a child's life. Notice that, at thirteen years old, these young people had already developed their convictions about what they would do in matters of purity. The early teen years are not the time to *start* the conversation. They are the time to put the finishing touches on a lengthy discussion that has already been happening since the child was very young. Training children early prepares young people properly when situations like this arise.

A second observation about this story is also worth noting. This daughter *talked* with her parents. She told them, in detail, what happened. For those without older children, this does not happen by chance. It happens because parents have cultivated an intimate and caring relationship with their children. How many of the other girls in this story told their parents about the same conversation? My guess is none. If this were your child, would she feel comfortable and safe to share the content of this conversation with you? What is the health of the relationship between you and your child? A good relationship between parent and child is critical in order for biblical truth to be embraced.

If your child had been at this sleepover, how would he or she have responded? Would your child have caved and eventually made ungodly choices? Would your child have been quiet and not stood up for the truth? Or would your child have held to strong biblical convictions?

Of course, we all want our children to have strong biblical convictions, but getting there is the challenge. The great news is that God has already provided us everything that we need for the task. My goal is to convey that to you in this book.

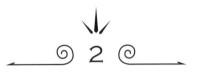

WHEN AND HOW
DO YOU BEGIN?

Starting Early with Scripture

Mark and Mary are unsure whether they should talk with their four- and six-year-old children about homosexuality. Recently the children noticed that their uncle lives with another man, and they have begun asking questions. Don's seven-year-old son has been intently watching cheerleaders on TV during football games, and Don wonders when he needs to start talking with his son about the opposite sex. Rosie's eight-year-old granddaughter came home talking about a crush on a boy from school. Rosie wonders whether it is normal for children this young to be thinking these thoughts.

Ryan and Claire heard that their friend's child accidentally stumbled onto a pornographic website while doing homework, and they are beginning to think they should address the issue with their own eight-year-old. Anne is married to a non-Christian husband and wants to make sure that she trains her sons to grow up to be godly husbands, but she doesn't know what to teach or when to start. Carrie, a single mom, sees her middle-school daughter gravitating toward the wrong kind of guys and is alarmed. She knows that she needs to talk with her daughter but is not sure what to say. Ethan and Taylor have a sixteen-year-old daughter who wants to go to a movie alone with a male friend from church. Ethan and Taylor feel pressure to say yes but haven't talked about the subject in depth with their daughter.

Chris and Abby, parents of three children under ten, approached me with a question that I am commonly asked: "When is it appropriate to talk to children about marriage, sex, and dating?" It was obvious they had given the question some thought, because they followed it up with a well-articulated chorus of concerns: "We are concerned that our children are too young, that the topic is too heavy and the content too deep, and that it would cause the children to worry about the state of our marriage."

I have had dozens of discussions with parents who are in situations like the ones above and are unsure what to do. Parents instinctively know that these are critical topics to talk about with children, but they tend to rationalize waiting until children are older to have the discussions.

In this chapter, we will explore what subjects you should address with your child and when you should begin to have those discussions.

The Biblical Pattern

What subjects related to marriage and sex should parents address with their children? The biblical guidance for all parents to remember is to *go where the Bible goes*. You can be confident and comfortable talking with your child about subjects that God addresses with children in the Bible. We've become timid in the twenty-first century about addressing hard topics with children, including sexuality. The pattern of Scripture is for parents and spiritual leaders to talk with children, sometimes with very young children, about the meaning of marriage, the biblical roles of husband and wife, and the purpose of sex, as well as adultery, homosexuality, incest, divorce, and sexual purity. Let's explore what the Bible says to children on these subjects.

In Joshua 8:35 we read, "There was not a word of all that Moses commanded that Joshua did not read before all the assembly of Israel,

38

and the women, *and the little ones*, and the sojourners who lived among them." Did you catch that? There was *not a word* of Moses' commands that Joshua did not read to the little ones. This prompts two questions: How old were the little ones? What are the words that Joshua read?

The Hebrew word for "little ones" refers to little children—those unable to march. The entire community—which included women, children, and foreigners—gathered to hear the law of God read. It was critical that every member know that he or she was under the same obligation to obey God's commands. Joshua did not want to repeat the rebellious mistake of the previous generation, so it was critical for the entire nation of Israel to obey God. Children were to observe and obey God's laws, while parents and grandparents were to love the Lord and impress these things on children.

What was read to the community? Joshua read all Moses' commands that were found in the first five books of the Bible to all Israel, including the children. When the Bible says, "There was not a word Moses commanded that was not read," I take that literally. Children would have listened as Genesis, Exodus, Leviticus, Numbers, and Deuteronomy were read—or, at minimum, the portions that included the commands of God.

In Joshua 8:35, we see that children are taught, from a young age, the comprehensive truths of Scripture. A quick scan through the first five books of the Bible reveals that young children were introduced to subjects that we typically reserve for older children or adults. Young children would have heard the definition of marriage in Genesis 2:24–25, the commandment against adultery in Exodus 20:14, and descriptions of forbidden sexual relations in Leviticus 18 (including incest, homosexuality, and bestiality), as well as stories involving polygamy (Gen. 12:10–20) and accusations of attempted rape (Gen. 39).

We can summarize Joshua 8:35 by saying that *all the commands of God are for all the people of God*—including men, women, and children. The nation of Israel did not shield their children from difficult portions of Scripture but taught the commands of God to their children with the end goal of having their children love God and obey him. Joshua 8:35 is, in some ways, the Old Testament's version of Acts 20:27: "For I did not shrink from declaring to you the whole counsel of God." Joshua declared the whole counsel of God to the whole people of God.

Go Where the Bible Goes

Many parents are fearful to declare the whole counsel of God to their children. Parents often reason that children are not developmentally ready to hear the full teaching of Scripture. Parents and pastors break from the biblical pattern when they teach limited portions of Scripture to children. Could it be that one reason young people are doctrinally ignorant, spiritually confused, and living with a syncretistic faith system is that we have reduced our teaching to the couple dozen moralistic stories found in most children's Bibles? Our children need the soul-gripping, life-altering, meat-based, Jesus-centered teachings of God's Word.

I recognize some people will object to the idea that children of all ages—young and old—should be taught all the truths of Scripture. But this isn't just a Joshua 8:35 concept. This concept is found throughout the entire Bible. Joshua, it appears, was imitating Moses' pattern of teaching all the people of God all the commands of God. In Deuteronomy 31:12 we read, "Assemble the people, men, women, and little ones, and the sojourner within your towns, that they may hear and learn to fear the LORD your God, and be careful to do all the words of this law." Moses conveys, almost word for word, the same idea as Joshua.

Later in the Old Testament, Nehemiah 8:1–3 tells us that "all the people gathered . . . both men and women and all who could understand what they heard. . . . And he read it [the book of the law of Moses] . . . from early morning until midday." This shatters a bit of the current developmental theory that children can listen for only short periods of time. Here, children listened to God's word being read from early morning until midday. Once again, they were introduced to the entire counsel of God. Maybe children can handle a bit more than we give them credit for.

Children in the Old Testament were exposed to a comprehensive reading of Scripture. When parents and leaders came to a difficult portion of Scripture, they did not excuse children from their midst or skip over it; they read it. And you should too. You can go, with your children, where God goes with children. You can read the entire Scripture to your children. This is the biblical pattern.

What Does the Bible Teach Children about Sex and Marriage?

God not only exposes children to a wide range of truth at early ages but also commands parents to teach children some specific truths related to marriage and sex.

In the Old Testament

In Deuteronomy 6:6–7, Moses commands parents and grandparents to diligently teach children the commands of God. Just what commands are parents to teach children? Are parents simply to teach children virtues and character traits? No—and the contents may surprise you. In Deuteronomy 5:6–21, Moses repeats the Ten Commandments. These were the commands that parents were to obey (6:3), place on their hearts (6:6), and teach diligently to children throughout the normal routine of the day (6:7). When Moses told parents to diligently teach their children, he had very specific content in mind: the Ten Commandments.

Most parents feel good about teaching their children to honor and obey them, not to steal, or not to lie (commandments five, eight, and nine). But parents are also commanded to teach their children the seventh and tenth commandments, "You shall not commit adultery" and "You shall not covet your neighbor's wife" (Deut. 5:18; 21). When was the last time you taught your child not to commit adultery? Does your child even know what adultery is? Most parents shy away from this subject with children. But, as we see, it is God's expectation that parents teach children faithfulness in marriage.

Parents, not only are you to expose your children to the life-giving truths of Scripture, you are also to diligently teach your children God's commands related to marriage and sex. An entire vein of parenting resources deals primarily with purity and puberty while ignoring the rest of Scripture. This is a problem. Somehow parents have been convinced that they need to wait before having serious talks with their children about serious subjects. This is simply not true, wise, or biblical. Is it any wonder that so many young people hold to unbiblical views of marriage and live in ungodly ways in regards to sex? The silence of parents has left many Christian children in the dark, exposed to the deception of the Enemy.

If Deuteronomy didn't convince you to address some difficult topics with your children—both young and old—then Proverbs should. The book of Proverbs was written by a parent to a child (see Prov. 1:8; 2:1; 3:1; 4:1; 5:1, 7; 6:1, 20; 7:1; 10:1) and deals with topics such as marriage, choosing a spouse, and purity. Proverbs 5–7 address some pretty sizzling topics. In God's wisdom, he recorded a father having "the talk" with his son. Not only this, but God recorded for us what we should talk about with our children. In Proverbs 5–7, the child is introduced to the female body (5:19), the role of sex in marriage (5:19), adultery (5:20), and prostitution (6:26). All told, roughly 10 percent of Proverbs deals with subjects that fall under the umbrella of marriage, sex, and purity. That is a lot of real estate in the only book of the Bible written specifically to children. And that should tell parents something about the importance of addressing these subjects.

In the New Testament

The New Testament has plenty to say to children about marriage, sex, and purity as well.

Children are addressed directly in Ephesians and Colossians (Eph. 6:1 and Col. 3:20). In these passages, Paul doesn't say, "Hey, parents, teach your children to obey you." He speaks directly to children. It would be no different from a pastor preaching a sermon and at some point directly saying to children, "Kids, listen up. I've got something to say specially for you: obey your parents."

For a young person to have heard, "Children, obey your parents," he or she would have had to be present, sitting with the rest of the congregation, listening to the entirety of Ephesians and Colossians. Along with the rest of the congregation, children were taught the biblical roles of husband and wife in marriage as well as the meaning and purpose of marriage (Eph. 5:22–33; Col. 3:18–19).

In the pastoral epistles, Paul tells older women that they are to teach younger women about marriage—especially about the role of a wife (Titus 2:5)—while older men are to teach younger men to control themselves—which has many applications for dating and marriage (Titus 2:6). In addition, Paul tells young Timothy to flee from sexual immorality (2 Tim. 2:22).

The pattern of Scripture is to teach children God's truths regarding marriage, sex, and purity. We can directly observe key passages, such as Genesis 2:24–25 and Ephesians 5:22–33, being taught to children—both young and old. Parents, there is no need to be unsure about the content you should talk about with your children. Just follow God's lead. Cover the topics that he covers with children. God doesn't sugarcoat tough topics. He doesn't avoid them. And neither should you. Parents can be confident about what to say, because their words should be a retelling of God's words. Read these key Scriptures with your children and discuss them. You don't have to create or find a marriage curriculum to discuss with your child. God has already provided that for you—it's the Bible.

When Should You Begin?

The Bible never provides a specific age to begin talking with your child about these issues, so there is flexibility based on the child, the family, the culture, and many other factors. However, while the Bible does not dictate a specific age, it does provide a pattern that I encourage parents to follow. The pattern is *early and often*. Paul says to

Timothy, "*From childhood* you have been acquainted with the sacred writings, which are able to make you wise for salvation through faith in Jesus Christ" (2 Tim. 3:15). The key principle here for us is that young people were taught the truths of Scripture "from childhood."

Our overall aim in teaching our children Scripture is their salvation through faith in Jesus. What is a critical component in securing this outcome? Teaching children the Scriptures from an early age. And if you systematically and regularly read through Scripture with your children, then you will come across Scriptures that speak to the subjects of marriage, sex, and purity.

Proverbs echoes a similar mind-set to 2 Timothy 3:15. Proverbs 4:3 states, "When I was a son with my father, tender, . . . he taught me." What did this father teach his young son? Proverbs 4:23–27 says that the father taught his young son four key truths about his body: protect your heart, control your mouth, be cautious with your eyes, and ponder your path (addressing his heart, mouth, eyes, and legs). This passage is full of applications regarding the subjects of marriage, dating, and purity. When did the father teach these things to his son? The author of Proverbs taught his son these important, and sometimes challenging, truths when the son was "tender," or young in age.

The author of Proverbs appears to have an "early and often" strategy for parenting. In Proverbs 22:6 we are told, "Start a child in the way he should go and when he is old he will not depart from it." This is not a guaranteed promise, but it's a principle that is true more often than not. How children start is often how they end. Teach a child from his earliest days, for all his days, God's design for marriage and for the roles of husband and wife, and it is likely that this child will embrace this teaching.

The Technology Challenge

Today's parents face an additional challenge that makes early -and-often teaching crucial. Thanks to electronic technology, in the form of social media, cell phones, television, and the Internet, children can turn on the television or search the Internet and be flooded with information about any subject, at any time.

In general, children are exposed to sexual information early, and access is easy. The Internet and television are without any secrets. Technology does not make age distinctions, and sexual images will be seen by anyone watching. Sexual innocence can quickly be lost in this environment.

This is exactly what happened to my children with a different subject: Star Wars. My children learned about Star Wars, not from seeing the movies, but from conversations with friends, ads, commercials, and toys. The Star Wars saturation of our culture piqued my children's curiosity and generated questions. My sons, without ever seeing the movies, knew their characters, key lines, and story.

What is true of Star Wars is also true of sex. It's everywhere. It saturates American culture. A parent and child can't walk through a checkout line at a grocery store without being confronted with immodestly dressed individuals on the covers of magazines. Just as my sons are being exposed to Star Wars, our children are being exposed to sex. This generates curiosity, raises questions, and necessitates action.

We live in a sex-saturated culture with 24/7 access to our children through technology, and that necessitates early and regular conversations with our children on subjects that previous generations could postpone until children were older.

Innocence but Not Ignorance

Let's return to Chris and Abby's concern about a subject being too heavy and deep for a young child to receive. The guideline I use as a parent and pastor, to teach both my children and other people's children, is to *aim for innocence but not ignorance*. It has taken me years to find the balance between giving children enough to prepare them to fight the good fight of faith in this area of life, but not so much that it awakens love before the proper time or places a weight on their shoulders that they cannot bear.

Children of all ages can be taught the meaning of marriage, the roles of husband and wife, and distortions of marriage such as divorce and homosexuality, as well as what to look for in a future spouse. How children are taught will differ based on age, but it is important to remember that God's message does not change based on age. Preschoolers and teenagers can both be taught that marriage is between one man and one woman. Peter Jeffery concurs.

> There is no doctrine in the Bible that Christian youngsters do not need to know and love. But there is a difference in teaching doctrine to a young people's fellowship and to a ministers' conference. The difference is not in subject matter but in depth and application. It is not a matter of watering down the doctrine to make it more acceptable but of explaining it in a way that makes it understandable to young believers.[1]

There is no biblical doctrine that children do not need to know. Do you believe that? The key is not to avoid a doctrine or water it down but to explain the doctrine in an understandable way.

What principles should a parent keep in mind in order to effectively teach the truth of Scripture to children, both young and old? That is the focus of the next chapter.

1. Peter Jeffery, *Bitesize Theology* (Grand Rapids: Evangelical Press, 2000), 11–12.

3

How to Communicate
with Your Child

The ABCs of Talking about
Marriage, Dating, and Sex

While parents may know *what* they are called to do (to bring up children in the Lord), the struggle lies in knowing *how* to prepare children for a gospel-centered life—especially when it comes to marriage, dating, and purity.

Ultimately, you should use the Bible as you train your child to grow up into a man or woman who loves Jesus and makes God-honoring decisions. But, as you begin to talk with your child about the subject matter of this book, following the ABCs of communication should help you to avoid major land mines and to create fruitful discussions.

Before we jump into the ABCs of talking about marriage, dating, and sex, one point must be made. The quality of your relationship with your child will likely determine your child's receptivity to your teaching. A relationship built on love and trust is necessary in order for a child to open his or her heart and take your words seriously. If your relationship with your child is not what you desire it to be, focus on strengthening it before discussing these matters. You may find it helpful to sit down and talk with a biblical counselor or a pastor in order to work through any problems using the Bible. Or you may want to have a conversation in which you express love for your child, ask for forgiveness, and commit to prioritize spending time with him or her. This may be just what you need in your relationship in order to lay a solid foundation for your instruction.

A: Accurate

Plenty of parents and teachers operate under the assumption that young children cannot handle the truth. Thus, they avoid or alter a subject in attempt to soften a truth.

A great example of this is seen in a Kia Super Bowl commercial, "Babylandia." When a young child asks his dad where babies come from, Dad's eyes grow as large as saucers. He has a choice: tell his son the truth, water it down, or fabricate something false. Unfortunately, he chooses the last option and describes a planet called Babylandia and the space-traveling babies that make a nine-month journey to their parents. The commercial ends when the son, who looks confused, responds, "But Jake says that babies are made when mommies and daddies—" He is abruptly cut off when the father commands his vehicle to play the song "Wheels on the Bus." This commercial is great entertainment but not good parenting guidance.

What is the damage if you withhold truth from your child?

- Your child is not given an accurate picture of reality.
- When your child finally learns the truth, your credibility takes a hit as your child naturally wonders whether you are trustworthy on other matters.
- By not telling your child the truth, you are encouraging him or her to seek the truth from other sources. Logically, if you are not providing a child with real, true, honest answers, why should he or she ask in the first place?

Plenty of children have asked me where babies come from. First I respond with Colossians 1:16: everything, including babies, is created by God and for God. That is enough for some young minds. But, if questions continue, I tell children that it takes a mommy and a daddy to make a baby and that a baby grows in a mommy's tummy and comes out after nine months. The book *Before I Was Born*[1] is a helpful tool to read when this question arises.

As you discuss matters of purity, marriage, and dating with your child, be accurate, be honest, and tell the truth. Call body parts by their correct names, share the truth with a child if he or she walks in on Mom and Dad during an intimate moment, and be honest with answers as questions arise. As much as possible, point a child to a Scripture passage so the child knows that truth and authority come from God, not from personal opinion.

I have two cautions.

First, some people are blunter than others. Make sure your encouragement is balanced with discernment. There should be a progression to what is said to children as they age. Avoid dumping everything on them at once.

Second, avoid gross detail and an alarmist approach. When addressing this topic with young people, some Christians use the tactic of talking in depth about STDs and pregnancy. While these consequences can be included in a discussion about the costs of sin, too much gory detail often shuts young people down. Stay high level and stay general, unless it is obvious that your child needs greater detail in a certain area.

B: Brief

When people take a thousand words to say what they could say in a hundred, what happens to your attention, focus, and application of their teaching? It is likely weakened.

We live in the era of sound bites and headlines. Television frames last one to two seconds before shifting to a new angle. Like it or not, your child has grown up on short, pithy forms of communication.

1. Carolyn Nystrom, *Before I Was Born*, rev. ed. (Pontiac, IL: NavPress, 2007).

This doesn't mean that we shouldn't expect our children to sit quietly and listen to a forty-minute sermon at church. It doesn't mean that they are unable to have long, fruitful discussions with others. But it does mean that, when you talk to your child, you need to be able to boil down to a sentence the message that you want him or her to take away from the conversation.

Don't take ten minutes to get to your main point. By then, you've probably lost your child's attention. Instead, know your main point in advance and get there quickly. (Just as I did in this paragraph!) If you can't do this, your message may be lost.

You should be able to concisely tell your child the biblical purpose of marriage, the roles of a husband and wife, and criteria for choosing a spouse. I'll help you with this in chapters 6, 8, 9, and 18. The rest of what you say to your child is commentary on the main point. It illustrates, clarifies, fleshes out, explains, and applies the central ideas. Children won't remember all the commentary. But they can remember one main point. That is the goal.

The Scriptures, and Jesus himself, model brevity. Thousands and thousands of pages have been written on marriage, dating, and purity. I have mountains of them in my study! Amazingly, however, the Bible explains marriage and purity in only a few words. The two primary passages on marriage—Genesis 2:24–25 and Ephesians 5:22–23—give us much of what we need in order to understand and live out a gospel-centered marriage. God accomplished his teaching in thirteen verses. We should keep this fact in the back of our minds as we train our children.

Many Christian resources unintentionally encourage parents toward what I call *dump truck parenting*. They encourage parents to take a child away for a weekend in order to discuss purity and puberty and to unload a large volume of information at once. My preference is regular, consistent discussion of marriage, dating, and purity throughout the child's life. Use these excellent resources as one step in a continual process of communication between yourself and your child—not as the totality of what a child will hear. In other words, have "the talks," not "the talk."

C: Correct Foundation

Each of us looks to someone or something as an authority on marriage. This determines what we believe about marriage and how we instruct our children to approach marriage. There are many sources that we look to for guidance, but I'm going to address three of the most common that I observe.

Your Parents' Marriage

Your parents' marriage was powerful. It shaped you. From its success or failure, you formed beliefs about what marriage is and how it should work. These beliefs may or may not be correct. And these beliefs are often held deep down in your core—so deep that you may never have thought about them critically or compared them to biblical teaching on marriage.

Too often, marriage patterns are created as we simply imitate or reject the example of our parents' marriage. This man-centered theology begins with a working or failing marriage and makes it the benchmark for our own marriages. A God-centered theology of marriage starts with the gospel and Jesus' covenant relationship with the church. That's a big difference. When you teach your children about marriage, start with Jesus, not with your parents.

Psychology

A lot of bad teaching about marriage is available today—and lots of it comes from well-intentioned Christian leaders. Many Christian parents use resources that are influenced more heavily by psychology than theology, leading to clouded understanding and theological confusion. What we teach our children will be incorrect if we base it on resources that are not biblically sound.

To be fair, psychology can provide valuable contributions that strengthen marriage. But the key to transformational teaching is to understand that Scripture is foundational and psychology is supplemental. If you know what God says on a subject, you will be able to detect and reject incorrect teachings and to appreciate and integrate the rest.

The Bible

The Bible has a lot to say about marriage. It is very clear and easy to understand. Clarity, confidence, and conviction will come when we take our directives about marriage from the Bible. Before picking up a book on marriage, pick up the Bible and find out what God himself has to say about the subject.

Few children have a settled conviction on, and clear understanding of, basic matters of faith and life. Why is this? Because few parents have strong biblical convictions or have succeeded in clearly communicating the Bible's truths to children. We need parents who say to their children, "This is what the Bible says—it may not be popular, but it is true." By God's grace, these parents will shape hearts and their children will make Jesus the Lord of their lives. The parent who says, "Well, I don't know . . ." or presents a buffet of views on a subject won't raise children with settled convictions.

Few things are more tragic than a wavering Christian. If you are not clear on a subject, your child will not be either. You cannot teach what you do not understand. It is critical that you know what the Bible teaches on divorce, homosexuality, transgenderism, cohabitation, polygamy, and more. Do you know what the Bible teaches about marriage in Genesis 2:24; Matthew 19; 1 Corinthians 6–7; Ephesians 5:22–33; Colossians 3:18–19; Titus 2; and 1 Peter 3:1–7? If not, these passages are the place to start.

D: Discussion Oriented

In addition to being accurate, brief, and centered on the Bible when you talk about marriage with your children, use questions to engage them in discussion, encourage their participation, and test their understanding.

Your goal is not simply to transfer a bunch of information from your brain to your child's brain. You are teaching for life transformation. For this to happen, you must engage and involve your child in critical thinking. Try following a three-step process with your child: read a short passage of Scripture, teach and/or discuss a biblical truth, and ask open-ended questions (questions that are not answered by a yes or no).

The only way to know what your child thinks, believes, questions, and desires is to give him or her the space and time to talk. You have specific content that you want to communicate with your child, but you can do this in a way that is interactive and engaging. At times, the child needs to listen quietly to what you say (isn't that the model that we see in the book of Proverbs?), but these times should be combined with two-way conversations and questions.

When you develop a strong relationship with a child, are honest and accurate about what you say, and invite questions from the child, you become an askable parent, grandparent, or teacher. We want the children in our care to ask us questions about marriage and dating rather than seek answers from other sources. Become skilled at asking and inviting questions and you will have a doorway into your child's heart.

E: Early and Often

I've already encouraged you to begin talking to your children about marriage, dating, and purity when they are young. Now I want to add two thoughts to what I have already said.

Think Slow Cooker, Not Microwave

When Colossians 1:28 discusses maturity, it uses *mature* to mean complete or full. It means ripeness of character. Maturity is Christlikeness. It is not instantaneous; it is a process that happens over a lifetime.

You may be saying, "Yeah, yeah; tell me something I don't know." The challenge is that we often expect our children to mature in a certain area quickly, and we get frustrated when we have similar conversations with them multiple times without seeing more noticeable growth. We know that growth takes time, but we want growth quickly. Notice the inconsistency?

This is why you need to think slow cooker, not microwave,

as you communicate truth to children. The best foods are cooked over low heat for a long time. When you commit to communicating God's truth to children early and often, you are committing to long-term communication on subjects that make a major difference in life. Don't think that you can have a one-and-done microwave conversation with your child on this type of subject and move on; this is not a successful approach to lifelong transformation.

Think Repetition

As parents, grandparents, or teachers, we will make a few one-time statements that our children will remember for the rest of their lives. But most of what will impact them deeply are things that we say over and over again, along with the way we live faithfully before their eyes. I continually say to my children, "Marriage is between one man and one woman for one lifetime, not between two men or two women." I trust that this phrase will come to mind when my children observe someone living a different lifestyle and will remind them that this is not God's best for that individual.

Repetition is important. It is a biblical method. Just read Proverbs 5–7. It is incredible how much time and space the father devotes to the adulterous woman. Proverbs 5 contains excellent teaching, but once wasn't enough. The father gives his son similar teaching in chapter 6 and again in chapter 7.

This method of communication catches my attention as a parent. Our children will hear the world's big lies at different ages and stages of their lives. Hearing the gospel truths of Scripture on marriage, dating, and purity at every stage will remind, defend, and guide the child's heart and help him or her to have strong biblical convictions.

F: First (and Loudest)

Our goal is to teach our children biblical truth before they hear the world's lie. Your child should be able to detect the lie and defend against it by using Scripture. This means that you need to be the first and loudest voice in your child's life. Don't let an unbiblical idea take root in your child's heart and slowly grow over time without detection. Instead, arm your children with the truth and help them to understand why the world's ideas are incorrect so that they can stand firm rather than be tossed about by the convincing arguments they will hear.

G: Greater Depth for Greater Maturity

How much should a parent tell a child about his or her sinful past? Knowing how much information to share with a child about past mistakes takes great discernment. We want our children to learn from our errors and avoid them, but we don't want to destroy our character or credibility in the process, nor do we want to glorify a past mistake.

The goal in sharing anything is to encourage a child to obey God and follow his ways. The following guidelines may be helpful:

- *Speak in generalities.* There is a big difference between saying that you went too far physically before marriage and sharing the details of that mistake.
- *Share greater detail for greater maturity.* Older children can handle more details and may ask for them. If the child is simply curious, there is no need to share. If sharing details will help the child to be holy, then it may be advantageous to share more. Your discernment is critical.
- *Emphasize consequences.* How do you help your children to understand marriage? Show them the results of sin. What did it cost? What were the hidden consequences that you didn't anticipate? It often appears to children that there are no consequences to sin and that everything turns out fine. The media glorifies sexual immorality while concealing the costs of sin. Let your children know that consequences did happen.

Josh McDowell has some great advice on communication that can be applied to talking about past mistakes. When it comes to what specifically we should teach our children, and at what ages, the operative principle is this:

> Little questions deserve little answers; big questions deserve big answers; and frank questions deserve frank answers. In other words, tailor what you teach to the age and actual question of the child. Loading down a child with too much information too soon can cause confusion and anxiety.[2]

H: Holistic

Much of the guidance from a previous generation of Christian experts encouraged parents to focus the bulk of discussion on the issues of puberty and purity. I don't know of many parents who get excited about the prospect of talking to children about biological changes, body parts, or sex. Unfortunately, many well-intentioned Christian experts counseled parents to reduce marriage preparation to a "say no to sex" campaign while talking about anatomy and reproductive systems. If that is the extent of the conversation between parent and child, I can understand why parents avoid the discussion or wait until the child is older.

Do parents need to talk with children about puberty and purity? Absolutely. But this should not be the extent of marriage preparation between a parent and child. Discussion needs to expand to include all that God teaches about marriage and about successful preparation for it. When this happens, a dreaded duty becomes a delightful discussion. Purity and puberty are woven into other discussions and fit under the grand umbrella of God's good design for marriage.

Beginning in the next section, I'll end each chapter with study questions and Scripture passages. My hope is that you will sit down with your child, read the passages out loud, study God's truths, and

---

2. Josh McDowell, *Why True Love Waits: The Definitive Book on How to Help Your Kids Resist Sexual Pressure* (Carol Stream, IL: Tyndale, 2002), 386.

discuss them together. I suggest that you cover one chapter at a time, at a pace that works for your family. You may want to study one chapter a week over a number of months or one chapter a month over the course of a year. If you have an older child, you may wish to read some portions of the book together, but in general the content of the chapters is intended for you. After studying God's Word together, you will be able to look for teachable moments and bring biblical truths into everyday conversations.

Ultimately your goal as you teach is for your child to grow as a follower of Jesus and be filled with love for him. How do you know whether you are a good teacher? Easy. Are your children learning? Are they being transformed into the likeness of Jesus? Are they living in obedience to God as described in the Bible? Try using the ABCs of talking about marriage, dating, and purity as you aim to effectively communicate with your children.

PART 2

MARRIAGE

An Overview of Marriage

Five Truths Every Child Must Know

Sandy approached me with tears in her eyes and asked to speak in private. She began the conversation by saying, "I need guidance," then paused to compose herself. Sandy explained that her son was planning to move in with his girlfriend. Her son said he had the "right to be happy" and wasn't seeking Sandy's approval, just her help. All he wanted was an extra pair of hands to move. It seemed like a reasonable request to him, but not to Sandy.

Sandy felt caught between showing compassion for her son and condoning something she did not agree with. "What do I do?" she asked me. "I believe what he is doing is wrong, but I'm not sure what to do. I never imagined he would live with someone before marriage." If you're wondering what I told Sandy to do, I told her to help her son move, but to make it clear that what he was doing was not pleasing to God. Relationships are the arteries that carry the gospel to our children. Sever the relationship and it affects our ability to influence our children with the gospel. In this instance, maintaining the relationship was critical, and that permitted helping her son move.

The above scenario is no longer uncommon. Children are growing up in a culture that encourages cohabitation, casual sexual encounters, divorce, and the redefinition of marriage. Parents rarely think that their children will embrace these cultural messages. No one wants to think that his or her child—who fervently prayed, sought the Lord, memorized Bible verses, went to church, and loved Jesus—might embrace an idea that leads him or her on a path away from Christ.

"I never imagined." Sandy's words stuck with me. It's unsettling to envision your child cohabitating or living in willful disobedience to God. As uncomfortable as it is, however, you should. Why? So that you do your part to help your child make wise, God-honoring choices. I've thought about what I would need to teach my children in order to help them establish biblical convictions and avoid a similar outcome, and I encourage you to do the same.

This is no small challenge—especially when an endless barrage of voices is trying to redefine marriage and tell our children to follow their feelings. The reality is that children make their own decisions. They will decide either to submit to God's authority or to live according to their own desires. I want to be able to say that I did everything I could to point my children to Christ. I don't want to be guilty of failing to train my children to conquer sexual temptation or "communicate the meaning and gospel significance of marriage."[1]

Let this warning motivate you to godly action and remind you of the importance of your role in nurturing your child's faith. Our goal is to help our children develop strong biblical convictions, and live according to them, so that cultural messages do not capture their affections and influence their decisions.

The first step toward accomplishing this outcome is to teach five biblical truths about marriage that every young person needs to know. Roll up your sleeves, sit down with your child, open the Bible, and let the Holy Spirit do his work through the living and active Word of God in the heart of your child.

---

1. "The Birds and the Bees: The Gospel and Your Child's Sexuality (Part 2)," The Ethics & Religious Liberty Commission of the Southern Baptist Convention, June 2, 2014, http://www.erlc.com/resource-library/articles/the-birds-and-the -bees-the-gospel-and-your-childs-sexuality-part-2.

Marriage Is Created by God

Every child needs to have a settled conviction about this truth: *God designed marriage, therefore God gets to define marriage.*[2] Understanding what marriage is begins with understanding where it came from.

I encourage you to read Genesis 2:22 in order to help young people understand the origin of marriage. Before reading this passage to your child, ask him or her if Adam and Eve were married—and, if so, who performed the wedding?

The answer: God did—because God created marriage! Genesis 2:22 says, "Then the LORD God made a woman from the rib he had taken out of the man, and he brought her to the man" (NIV). Lots of people read this passage and skip over it, not realizing the importance of these words. It tells us that marriage exists because God brought two people together. Marriage was God's idea. God caused Adam to fall asleep, and then he took a rib, made woman, and brought her to the man. The words "brought her to the man" are the Bible's way of saying, "I now pronounce you man and wife." The first wedding ceremony in the history of the world was officiated by God.[3]

If you're not convinced, Genesis 3 should help. In this chapter we are told that Eve ate the fruit she had taken and "also gave some to her *husband*" (v. 6). Then we are told that "the man and his *wife* hid" (v. 8). The Bible recognizes Adam and Eve as husband and wife immediately following Genesis 2:22.[4]

God's first priority, following the creation of the world, was the creation of marriage. Marriage was of *first* importance on God's to-do list. And it should be of first importance for us to get it right with our kids.

2. Adapted from comments made by Troy Dobbs, Senior Pastor of Grace Church of Eden Prairie.

3. Every time a father gives his daughter away in marriage, he imitates God the Father, who gave Eve to Adam.

4. The newlywed couple had quite the honeymoon in Genesis 3. Talk about a rocky start to a marriage. The good thing is, if Adam and Eve's marriage could survive the lies of Satan and the fall of man, every marriage has a fighting chance!

One of the most critical truths that every child must deeply believe is that marriage is God's creation—and that means that God has the authority to determine what marriage is and what it is not. This guards against culture's attempt to erode the foundation and redefine the institution. As we will see later in more detail, the account in Genesis is not just a *description* of a kind of marriage but God's *prescription* for all future marriages.

Marriage Is for God's Glory

If God created marriage, then the natural question that follows is: why? He must have a purpose for it. What is marriage meant to accomplish? Ask your child this question.

Most people get married hoping that their marriage will accomplish something. They might get married for companionship, happiness, financial security, physical and emotional intimacy, or children. The problem is that these reasons (while good desires) have everything to do with them and little to do with God. A godless society has made marriage into a godless entity. Society has made marriage into a man-centered, needs-based relationship that emphasizes romantic feelings of love from one person to another.

This perspective can easily influence our children. If marriage has nothing to do with God, then it has everything to do with the married couple. Marriage becomes about the couple's happiness, romance, and adventure. If romance fizzles or adventure fades, then the couple begins to think that maybe the marriage is over. Maybe it was a mistake to begin with. When people believe that marriage is fundamentally about them, their orientation is to seek their own happiness.

This entire perspective is wrong, and our kids need to hear this loud and clear. Marriage has everything to do with God and little to do with them. Colossians 1:16 states that "all things were created through him and for him." This includes marriage. Marriage is *from* God and *for* God. It was given by God to man as a gift, and—like all gifts—marriage has the potential to take the place of the gift giver and be used in the wrong way. When a marriage exists solely for a person's pleasure or happiness, it has become something that God never intended it to be. Marriage was created to be others-centered, not self-centered. Your child's eventual marriage should be selfless, not selfish. *Marriage is to be motivated by the desire to please God.*

Work hard to ensure that your child does not allow happiness to become the driving motive for marriage or the grid by which your child makes decisions in a future marriage. The great irony is that your child will be happiest and his or her marriage will be healthiest when your child lives to please God. Teach your child to make decisions that honor God by doing what he requires. This includes:

- *big things*, such as dating and marrying only a Christian.
- *mundane things*, such as learning to forgive when wronged and to communicate in a way that is pleasing to God (Eph. 4:29 is a great passage for every child to memorize).
- *foundational things*, such as (for girls) learning to manage a home or (for boys) learning to lead a family spiritually.

Pleasing God means doing all these things and more.

Ultimately, marriage exists as a means to display the gospel for God's glory. We'll talk a lot more about this in the next chapter, so I'll focus here on what it means to help our children learn to glorify God. To glorify God is to live in such a way that God's character is revealed and that praise for his name increases. Marriage is meant to do that. Every marriage is commissioned with the task of telling the story of the cross. Teach your child that, as people watch a self-sacrificing, others-centered, servant-minded marriage, it reminds them of Jesus' sacrificial love for us. And this glorifies God.

Marriage Is Good

We are told that some in the Ephesian church "for[bade] marriage" and taught that singleness was a greater form of spirituality. Paul combatted this aesthetic mind-set by responding that "God

65

created everything to be received with thanksgiving. . . . For everything God created is good and nothing is to be rejected" (1 Tim. 4:3–5). Marriage is good, and your job is to *enthusiastically champion marriage to your child*. Practically, this means you should speak positively about marriage to your child the same way the Bible speaks positively about marriage.

Negative views of marriage are common. You need to guard against such views taking hold in your child's heart. John Piper writes, "There has never been a generation whose general view of marriage is high enough. . . . Some, like our own, have such low, casual, take-it-or-leave-it attitudes toward marriage as to make the biblical vision seem ludicrous to most people."[5] I've observed three ways in which children develop negative perceptions of marriage.

- *Negative example due to a struggling marriage.* Crumbling marriages leave children to wonder if marriage works. Why get married at all, they wonder, if marriage will end poorly and cause pain? It is tempting to remain single and get all the perceived benefits of marriage without the commitment. If a dissolving marriage has touched your home, you may have to work extra hard on this one. Experience is a powerful teacher—if a child's experience is negative, then the perception of marriage can easily be the same. Remind your child that his or her experience of marriage, good or bad, does not determine its value. For that, we look to Scripture.
- *Negative attitude expressed in complaints.* A negative view of marriage develops over time when the majority of what a child hears about marriage comes in the form of complaints and sarcasm. It's easy to complain about a spouse without even realizing it, and children pick up on this. For example, have you heard someone refer to marriage as "the old ball and chain"? Is it any wonder that children think poorly of

5. John Piper, *This Momentary Marriage: A Parable of Permanence* (Wheaton, IL: Crossway Books, 2012), 19.

marriage when married people refer to it as a prison sentence? In Proverbs 5:18, a boy is instructed by his father to "rejoice in the wife of his youth." The key word is *rejoice*. Spouses are commanded to express gladness with one another. Your child should be hearing praise for your spouse coming from your mouth, not complaints.

- *Negative teaching about sex.* In a well-intentioned effort to teach children the limitations and purpose of sex, parents can fail to communicate its beauty and joy within the context of marriage. Make it your goal to paint a strong contrast between sex that is good and godly and sex that is immoral.

Be careful not to always give negative examples of sex, speak with a negative outlook on marriage, or teach a negative view of marriage. Instead, continually give yourself to the task of elevating and celebrating marriage in your home so that marriage is desirable to your child.

Marriage Is the Expected Norm

Statistics reveal that cohabitation is on the rise and that young people are marrying later in life than previous generations did. This tells me that high numbers of young people believe that it's better to remain single rather than get married. Some people have God's calling in their lives to remain single (1 Cor. 7:7). Biblically, singleness is a gift as well as marriage is. If that is God's plan for your child, it is to be gladly received and intentionally embraced for the Lord. I will talk more about this in chapter 10.

Most young people should plan to get married in God's timing. You can communicate this biblical expectation to your child by reading and discussing Genesis 2:18. God spoke the pattern of marriage into existence when he said, "It is not good for man to be alone" (Gen. 2:18). This statement is directed toward all people, including your child.

Help your child to recognize that longings for children or for sex are longings for marriage—the context in which God has designed for both to occur. Most people have God-given sexual desires and, according to the Bible, the existence of these desires in our children may be God's encouragement for them to marry. First Corinthians 7:9 states that it is better to marry than to sin sexually. Unless God has given your child the ability to control physical urges, it is good for him or her to get married.

Marriage Is a Covenant

We live in a time when unfaithfulness is common and commitment is conditional. Therefore, it is critical that our children have a strong biblical conviction on this point: that nothing will separate them from a future spouse but death. That is the biblical concept of a covenant, and it could be the difference between an adult child's marriage ending in divorce or lasting until the death of a spouse. You can help to affair-proof and divorce-proof your child's marriage by teaching your child that marriage is a *make-it-and-never-break-it promise.*

In the Bible, marriage is called a *covenant*—a very serious, unbreakable promise patterned after God's promise to us. (We'll explore this more in chapter 6.) We see this in Malachi 2:14 when the prophet states, "The LORD was witness between you and the wife of your youth . . . she is your companion and your wife by covenant."

God loves to attend weddings! He will attend your child's wedding—not as a passive observer but as a witness. When a bride and groom exchange vows, they do so before God. This means that marriage is not merely a human agreement but a relationship under God.

When do a couple officially become husband and wife? Is it when they consummate the marriage? The answer has to be no, because then we would be married to anyone we were physically intimate with. Is it when the government officially records the marriage license? Again the answer has to be no. If marriage is established by a piece of paper, then it can be dissolved the same way. Jesus teaches that marriage is God-sealed: he joins husbands and wives together (Mark 10:8–9). I believe that this happens when vows are exchanged.

This is an important point, because what is God-sealed cannot be humanly undone. Covenants are serious. Nothing but death should separate husband from wife. Because of this, lifelong marriage should be entered into carefully.

Children are growing up in a culture that tells them that cohabitation and casual sexual encounters are good. They are living at a time when American culture is attempting to redefine marriage. Like Sandy's son at the beginning of the chapter, children are in danger of embracing these powerful messages. These five truths, carefully taught and consistently modeled, are the beginnings of a solid foundation for a Christ-centered marriage. They will help our children reject the counterfeit claims of culture and develop biblical convictions.

Courageous Conversations

1. Do you see yourself getting married one day? Why or why not?
2. Have you ever been to a wedding? If so, what does a wedding symbolize?
3. Read Genesis 2:22. Where did marriage come from? Were Adam and Eve married or cohabitating? If they were married, who performed the wedding?
4. Read Genesis 3:6–8, emphasizing the words "husband" and "wife."
5. God created marriage for a purpose. What is one purpose for marriage, according to Colossians 1:16?
6. Read 1 Timothy 4:4–5 and Proverbs 5:18. How do these two passages describe marriage? As a result, what is to be our view of marriage?
7. The Bible tells us in Genesis 2:18 that it is not good for man to be alone. Let's say that with your name in place of the word

man: It is not good for _____ to be alone. This means that it may be God's plan for you to be married.

8. Read 1 Corinthians 7:7. What does Paul mean when he talks about wishing that everyone were "as I am"?

9. According to Malachi 2:14, marriage is a covenant. What is a covenant and why is this important?

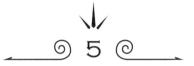

WHAT IS MARRIAGE? (PART 1)

Marriage Is for One Man and One Woman

When it comes to teaching children about marriage, where do you start? We have already established that marriage should be taught from the Bible—but the Bible is a big book, and it has a lot to say about marriage. Knowing where to start can be challenging.

When I was teaching a seminar on this topic to parents, one father admitted that he didn't know the Bible as well as he would like to. He understood the need to nurture his child's faith in this area of life and was motivated to get started, but he saw a mountain of information with no path forward. He wanted a bite-sized plan.

Another parent expressed a fear of saying or doing the wrong thing. "After all," she said, "my parents never did anything like this with me. As a child, I had to figure all this stuff out on my own." Without a good model, this mom was left to feel her way through her first-time parenting experience. She wanted an example.

On top of this, parents of young children have had it ingrained in them that certain biblical topics are inappropriate to talk about with kids. As a result, many parents don't start thinking about marriage, dating, and purity until their oldest child enters the mid-elementary years. When I show them that the Bible gives them permission to have these conversations with their children, many parents feel they have some catching up to do. Urgency manifests itself in the question "Where do I start?"

If you identify with any of these parents, you aren't alone. This chapter will point you in the right direction.

Begin with Genesis 2:24

Where does the Bible define marriage by stating, "Marriage is _____?" The definition of marriage is in the Bible, but it is often missed because God built the definition of marriage into a narrative portion of Scripture. The principles of marriage are delivered in the form of a narrative history lesson in Genesis 2. In this history lesson, Adam is created, God commands him not to eat from the Tree of Knowledge of Good and Evil, Adam names the animals, Eve is created, and Adam and Eve are married.

Take a moment and glance through Genesis 2:20–24.

> For Adam there was not found a helper fit for him. So the LORD God caused a deep sleep to fall upon the man, and while he slept took one of his ribs and closed up its place with flesh. And the rib that the LORD God had taken from the man he made into a woman and brought her to the man. Then the man said,
>
> "This at last is bone of my bones
>   and flesh of my flesh;
> she shall be called Woman,
>   because she was taken out of Man."
>
> Therefore a man shall leave his father and his mother and hold fast to his wife, and they shall become one flesh.

I encourage you to read this passage out loud with your child, invite your child to find where God defines marriage, and discuss the definition together. Why begin with Genesis 2:24? There are three reasons.

- *God introduces marriage in Genesis 2:24.* It is wise to begin teaching children about marriage where God begins teaching it to us.
- *Genesis 2:24 is the most quoted verse on marriage in the Bible.* New Testament writers reference it, Jesus quotes it, and Paul highlights it when he speaks of marriage (Matt. 19:5; Mark 10:7; Eph. 5:31). Remove this verse and we have eliminated an important scriptural foundation for marriage.
- *Genesis 2:24 is God's definition of marriage.*

Perhaps you're wondering whether Genesis 2:24 serves as a broad definition of marriage. Maybe it just describes Adam and Eve's relationship. But notice a couple of things. First, Genesis 2:22, not Genesis 2:24, describes Adam and Eve's marriage. When the Bible states that God brought Eve to Adam, this is equivalent to a wedding ceremony. Second, Adam and Eve didn't leave their father and mother, because they didn't have biological parents. Third, the Bible shifts from talking about Adam and Eve specifically to humans generally when it shifts from Adam's words in verse 23 to God's words in verse 24. Verse 24 is a comment from the Creator about the establishment of marriage. It's as if God concludes the story by saying, "What just happened with Adam and Eve—that's marriage. And it is an example of what I expect for all future marriages."

Genesis 2:24 is God's universal definition of marriage—it applies to all people, in every generation, everywhere in the world. Genesis 2:24 is God's way of saying, "Marriage is _____."

God created marriage, which means he gets to define it. We don't have to look to majority consensus, social scientific research, personal experience, or the Pope to understand what marriage is. God's definition is clear, concise, and timeless. It comes at the beginning of the Bible, revealing its importance in Scripture and in the created order. *Your goal is for God's definition of marriage to become your child's definition of marriage.*

What is God's definition of marriage? According to Genesis 2:24, marriage is *one man and one woman for life.* No other form of marriage is blessed in the Bible.

In the next chapter, I'll get into what "for life" means. For now, let's focus on what it means for marriage to be between one man and one woman.

One Man, One Woman

Recently one of my children asked a "What is marriage?" question. The question seemed to come out of nowhere. I was cooking eggs for breakfast, and my five-year-old son wandered into the kitchen. He greeted me and gave me a big smile. He told me he had a great night's sleep. Then, as coolly as if he were asking what time it was, he asked me, "Dad, can people marry dogs?"

"What a great question," I replied. "Did you know that a woman in England just married her dog? Another woman married her TV. And another woman married herself." My son's eyes and mouth told me he was surprised. "The short answer is no. Wanna know why? Because God created marriage to be between a man and a woman, not between a human and a dog."

Most people would consider marriage between a human and an animal to be abnormal. But why? Most would consider marriage between a human and an electronic device to be bizarre. How come? Why is it considered odd to marry yourself? If marriage can be anything we want it to be, then these forms should be acceptable. But since God defined marriage, we can know what it is and also recognize what it is not.

As the creator of marriage, God alone has the right to determine what marriage is and isn't. Genesis 2:24 indicates that marriage is between one man and one woman. Genesis introduces the idea, the Old and New Testament writers reinforce it, and Jesus reiterates it verbatim, meaning there is not a time stamp on this idea. Nowhere in the Bible is any other combination of genders or number of participants encouraged or endorsed. God made one helper for Adam, and she was female. We are told that *a* man is to marry *a* woman. Any other form of marriage does not fit this pattern.

How do you communicate this to a child? I tell my own children that, if you are a boy, God intends for you to marry a girl. If you are a girl, God intends for you to marry a boy. Pretty simple.

Marriage is not done morphing in our society, so it is critical for our children to know the truth in order to spot the error. Counterfeit forms of marriage will continue to surface, such as plural marriage, open marriage, and incest. Because God defines marriage in Genesis 2:24, we can identify all counterfeit forms of marriage with ease. When our children are confronted with these expressions of marriage, they can evaluate them based on this verse.

Addressing Homosexuality

Imagine that you are having a discussion with your child about the definition of marriage. During the conversation, you state that marriage is not meant to be between two men or two women. You can tell that your child is uneasy about this idea, and he or she responds by saying that the Bible doesn't say anything against homosexuality. Let's assume that your child is a genius, because of course he or she is. Your child claims that some references to homosexuality, such as Leviticus 18:22, were specific only to that culture and that some references were speaking against unethical sexual practices in general (i.e., 1 Cor. 6:9–11). Is that true? How do you respond?

Let's just assume, for the sake of this discussion, that the Bible doesn't say anything specific about homosexuality (even though it does—see Romans 1:24–28). That wouldn't be a problem, because the Bible very clearly tells us what marriage is. In Mark 10:6, Jesus states, "From the beginning of creation, God made them male and female." God created two genders for a reason, and the application is found in Mark 10:7 (a quotation of Genesis 2:24): "Therefore *a man* shall leave his father and mother and hold fast to his *wife*." Homosexuality is a drastic departure from the biblical model of marriage at almost every point.[1]

1. See Andreas J. Köstenberger and David W. Jones, *God, Marriage, and Family: Rebuilding the Biblical Foundation*, 2nd ed. (Wheaton, IL: Crossway Books,

Because homosexuality has become culturally acceptable, children must know what the Bible teaches on this subject. I encourage you not to be timid on this point with your child. Some parents are tempted to avoid this topic because of cultural pressure. I get it. However, silence on a subject is never the answer. Silence does two things: it communicates agreement and it abdicates to others. Silence teaches plenty. If you don't provide a clear definition of marriage from the Bible, someone else will, and it likely won't be biblical.

Coming under God's Moral Law

Why is it so important to teach the one-man-one-woman aspect of marriage? Why does it even matter?

The Bible is not a buffet of moral options from which our children can choose what they like and don't like. God is the authority for right and wrong. Unless your child believes this in faith and receives it in full, he or she will be at great risk of straying from God. Let us echo the psalmist's prayer for our children: "Open my eyes, that I may behold wondrous things out of your law" (Ps. 119:18). God's ways are wonderful and good. They are a delight to follow because they bring joy and blessing.

Teaching children that marriage is between one man and one woman is teaching children to come under the authority of God's Word. A low view of Scripture will lead to a low view of marriage. Avoid defining marriage based on your personal preference or lifestyle choice; rather, align your lifestyle with God's design for marriage. The key issue is the authority and trustworthiness of the Bible. What our children believe about the Bible will inform what they believe about marriage. It is important to establish the Bible's authority (that it tells us how to live), inerrancy (that it has no errors in its original manuscript), and sufficiency (that it is enough) with our children.[2]

2010), 200–201.

2. Expanding on these aspects of the Bible in regard to the topic of homosexuality is beyond the scope of this book. But if you want a resource to help toward

Additionally, if your child has a tendency toward gender confusion, it is absolutely critical that he or she understand what marriage is. Society encourages children to explore gender options. God's boundaries for relationships remind young people that if they are attracted to members of the same sex, this is a spiritual battle that must be fought, not an area of self-indulgence to explore.

If our children misunderstand marriage, they are prone to misunderstand the nature and character of God. At its core, marriage is about God. In it, we get a glimpse of who God is. Marriage reminds us of God's sacrificial love through Jesus' death on the cross. We see that Jesus came to serve, not to be served. Jesus sets the standard for faithfulness in marriage when he tells his bride, the church, "Never will I leave you or forsake you" (see Heb. 13:5). Sacrifice, service, faithfulness—these are the very things we are to live out in marriage. If you think it is important for your child to understand who God is, then it is important for your child to understand what marriage is. Or, to put it a different way, a distorted picture of marriage presents a distorted picture of the gospel. Anything that touches on the gospel should be of critical importance to you as a parent.

Convictional Kindness

When I teach my children on this subject, I also teach them to have *convictional kindness.* Convictional kindness is another way of teaching children to balance grace and truth. Take away one or the other, and problems surface. Take away grace, and you get a Christian who communicates truth in an unloving or condemning way. Take away truth, and you get hollow love that won't help someone in the end.

In this chapter, I've emphasized teaching the convictional side of things. Your child must learn what is true, right, and good. He or she needs to have deep-down convictions. But it is not enough to teach

---

that end, I commend to you Kevin DeYoung's book *What Does the Bible Really Teach about Homosexuality?* (Wheaton, IL: Crossway, 2015).

your child truth. You must also teach your child how to interact with others on this subject in a way that is loving and kind—a way that represents Christ well.

Our culture is trying to revise biblical sexuality and redefine marriage. God's definition of marriage is uncompromising and unalterable. Let us teach this to our children, with conviction and with kindness, so that they can do the same for others.

Courageous Conversations

1. Ask your child to share his or her definition of marriage. If your child struggles to answer, ask him or her to complete the sentence, "Marriage is _____."
2. Challenge your child to find where the Bible defines marriage and what that definition is. Give your child a few minutes to look through the Bible and come up with an answer.
3. Read Genesis 2:22–25. What is the definition of marriage according to Genesis 2:24? Finish this sentence, according to Genesis 2:24: "Marriage is _____."
4. Read Mark 10:6–7. What is the definition of marriage according to Jesus?
5. Read Ephesians 5:31. What is the definition of marriage according to Paul?
6. Why is it important to know God's definition of marriage? What limitations does this have regarding who you should or should not marry?
7. According to the following passages, who is marriage *not* for?
   a. Romans 1:26–27
   b. Leviticus 18:22
   c. 1 Corinthians 6:9–11
8. A friend of yours mentions that he sees nothing wrong with homosexuality. How would you respond?

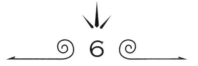

6

WHAT IS MARRIAGE? (PART 2)

Marriage Is a Lifelong Covenant

Andrew's parents are divorced. Before they separated, his home was a war zone with constant fighting. From Andrew's perspective, marriage is messy and messed up. Everywhere he looks, people seem to be divorced or in a struggling marriage. Andrew wonders why anyone would want to get married if it's going to be hard and likely end badly.

Andrew isn't alone. His parents didn't enter into marriage expecting to get divorced, yet high numbers of Christian marriages end this way.

During my PhD research, I had the privilege of talking with men and women all over the country about their role as grandparents. Almost a quarter of the grandparents I spoke with had at least one divorced adult child. Their voices could not hide the heartache they felt as they described the emotional and spiritual fallout for their grandchildren. As I listened to them talk, I pondered how I could help my children and other people's children avoid a similar fate.

Before We Start

You may have experienced divorce firsthand as a spouse or as a child. In all likelihood, you have a divorced friend or family member.

Maybe your marriage is struggling right now and you are considering divorce. Whatever your experience may be, it will likely affect how you read this chapter.

Know that, as I write this chapter, I am not condemning anyone who has experienced divorce. I'm writing so that our children can be taught the life-giving words of Scripture. Let me say three things up front so that this chapter is helpful for you.

- *Try not to let your personal experience become your authoritative source of truth.* My hope is that you will objectively consider what the Bible says on this subject without being unnecessarily influenced by your experience.
- *If you feel agitated while reading this chapter, determine whether you are being condemned or convicted.* One way to recognize the difference between the two is to consider where each leads. Condemnation proclaims you are a failure and points out a problem without providing a solution. It leads to shame and often causes a person to inflict self-punishment. Conviction from the Holy Spirit causes godly sorrow and invites you to repent of sin. It leads to Christ, who offers to take your punishment and declare you free from guilt. Satan condemns, so a feeling of condemnation is not of the Lord (John 3:17). But God's moral standards are convicting. If God's Spirit convicts your heart, recognize this and respond appropriately.
- *Know that any parent can teach the truths in this chapter, regardless of past experiences.* If you've messed up, let your child know it. Each of us makes mistakes in front of our children in many areas of life. Can we no longer teach our children because we've fallen short of God's standard? No—but we start by telling our children that we blew it. We confess that we haven't been living as God commanded, and, if appropriate, we talk about the consequences of sin. Our response to sin is crucial for our children. Explain to your child that you don't want him or her to experience the same things that

you did. Tell your child that, while wise people learn from their mistakes, wiser people learn from the mistakes of others. Your godly sorrow, and a repentant heart that leads to obedient living, will make an impact on your child, teaching him or her how to respond to sin and pointing him or her to the cross.

Our culture does not encourage unconditional commitment, so your child needs to hear from you on this subject. Will you teach your child that a marriage promise is unconditional? As we'll see, this is what the Bible teaches.

Marriage Is for Life

Holding Fast

In the last chapter, we looked at how Genesis 2:24 shows us that marriage is to be between one man and one woman. It also shows us that marriage is to last a lifetime. When Genesis 2:24 says that the husband and wife are to "hold fast" to one another, it is saying that marriage is for life. To "hold fast" means to be glued together. It is a bonding so close that two separate individuals become one. Oneness is to define the relationship.

There are lots of applications to this point. A married couple should have oneness spiritually, physically, financially, and emotionally. Couples should strive to do all things as one: sleep in the same bed, have one bank account, share the same biblical approach to parenting—they should not have separate lives, separate churches, or separate gods. Oneness in both the little and big things of life fuels a healthy marriage. Separation in certain places in a marriage tends to spread to other areas, and it often ends in the final separation of divorce. Our children need to be taught to develop and maintain oneness in marriage, as this will help them to "hold fast" to their spouses for life.

The word translated *hold fast* has another meaning. To hold fast is not just to glue two people together but to connect bone to skin.

I like to ask children, "Would it be painful to remove your skin from your bones?" Of course it would! This is a graphic reminder of how painful it is to go from oneness in marriage to separation through divorce.[1]

If you teach children, this mere mention of glue has probably sparked ideas for an object lesson. One particularly useful object lesson, which I've used with young people of all ages, is to glue together two pieces of construction paper—one blue and one pink. This gives a visual definition of marriage: *one man* (the blue construction paper) and *one woman* (the pink construction paper) *for life* (glued together). After you teach through Genesis 2:24, ask your child to separate the glued construction paper. The result? Chunks of paper come off with the blue and pink paper still attached to one another.

Divorce is never a clean break. It is difficult and painful.

Not Separating

Jesus says, "What God has joined together, let no one separate" (Matt. 19:6). If we take this literally, it sets a very high standard for marriage.

How do you respond to Jesus' statement? The Jewish leaders didn't like it. They thought it was too restricting—maybe even impossible. They thought divorce should be permitted in certain instances. To make their case, they appealed to Moses and asked Jesus, "If what you say is true, how come Moses allowed divorce?" (see v. 7).[2] (I can hear the Jewish leaders now: "Explain that one for us, Jesus!")

1. Sometimes it helps to be reminded what those hurts are. If you are looking for specifics, Judith S. Wallerstein, Julia M. Lewis, and Sandra Blakeslee studied the impact of divorce on children and wrote about their findings in the book *The Unexpected Legacy of Divorce: The 25 Year Landmark Study* (New York: Hachette Books, 2001). They interviewed the same individuals as children and then as young adults. Their research showed that the impact of divorce is lifelong and extremely formative in a negative way. Children move on, but they never fully recover as adults.

2. They were referencing Deuteronomy 24:1–4, in which Moses made allowance for divorce.

In response to their difficult question, Jesus said, "Because of your hardness of heart Moses allowed you to divorce your wives" (v. 8). In other words, divorce was the lesser of two evils.

However, Jesus didn't end there. He also said, at the end of the same verse, "But from the beginning [Genesis 2:24] it was not so." Referring back to Genesis, Jesus made the point that Moses didn't establish a pattern but deviated from it. God's original design for marriage had not changed. He still expects marriage for life as his standard. The lifelong marriage established by God at the start of the Old Testament was affirmed by Jesus in the New.

The response of the disciples to Jesus' teaching on lifelong marriage is noteworthy. They were shocked. This was such a hard teaching that the disciples asked Jesus if it was better never to marry (Matt. 19:10). Our children may wonder the same thing. Andrew did. The rise of cohabitation and the decline of marriage rates indicate that plenty of young people are thinking similar thoughts. It may be good to remind your child that cohabitation is ambiguous as it provides no clear definition to the relationship, it is uncertain due to low levels of commitment, and it is sinful as it clearly violates God's sexual limitations. Research reveals that couples who cohabitate have higher levels of divorce and depression as well as lower levels of relational satisfaction and stability. In addition, cohabitation leads to a higher probability of children being born out of wedlock and single-parent homes. Cohabitation is not God's method for testing for relational compatibility or preparation for marriage.

Raising Godly Children

One of the strongest deterrents against divorce is found in Malachi 2:15: "Did he not make them one [speaking of marriage], with a portion of the Spirit in their union? And what was the one God seeking? Godly offspring. So guard yourselves in your spirit, and let none of you be faithless to the wife of your youth."

Marriage is the artery that carries the gospel to children; in Malachi's words, one of its purposes is to produce godly offspring.

Severing the artery impacts the delivery of the gospel, meaning that divorce may produce *ungodly* offspring.

Sometimes, when I'm counseling a couple who are considering divorce, I ask them, "Would you get a divorce if you knew it meant that your child was going to reject Jesus and spend eternity without him?" That's a heavy question. I don't ask it flippantly. The Bible teaches that the pain of divorce not only touches us in this life but may stretch into eternity. That is meant to motivate us to faithfulness.

Three Things to Teach Your Child about Covenants

God designed marriage to be permanent. It is more than a relationship between two people; it is a portrait of Jesus Christ and his covenant relationship with the church. As you teach your child about marriage, here are three things that he or she should know about covenants. These things provide the backbone for commitment in marriage.

Making a Covenant Is Serious

In Bible times, when two people entered into a covenant, they would kill a lamb or a goat and cut its body in half. The two halves would be laid on the ground, and the people making the covenant would finalize their promise by walking between the two halves and saying, "May God do so to me [i.e., cut me in half] if I ever break this covenant with you and God." A man and woman are to enter into marriage with this level of seriousness.

Vows are not empty words. Your child shouldn't get married unless the vows are as unbreakable in his or her mind as they are in God's. Will your child really mean the words of this vow? For richer or poorer? In sickness and health? In good times and bad? Till death do you part? Or is his or her commitment conditional on good health, good wealth, good habits, and good times? Marriage is to be entered into with much thought and in accordance with biblical principles. No other decision in life, short of faith in Christ, affects a person nearly as much.

Covenants Ought to Be Permanent

God never breaks a covenant in the Bible. Never. Not once.[3] For those who have a sincere faith in Christ, God's promise of salvation is always honored, despite the sinful practices of his people (for example, see Hosea 2:16–20 and Psalm 89:34). The Bible makes it abundantly clear that we are an adulterous people who "turn to other gods" and "are bent on turning away from God" (Hosea 3:1; 11:7). Like an unfaithful spouse, we have each given our love to someone or something other than God. And we do this again and again and again. Every time we sin, we can classify it as spiritual adultery against God. We are repeatedly, habitually, willingly unfaithful to God. Thank God that his love for us is not dependent on our perfection or performance (Eph. 1:4)!

How does God respond to our unfaithfulness? How does God respond to a bride who is bent on loving the wrong things? How does God respond to a stiff-necked and rebellious people? He says, "Never will I leave you or forsake you" (Deut. 31:6; Heb. 13:5). Those aren't conditional words. That's a promise. And it is one that God will not break.

What does this have to do with marriage? Marriage is patterned after God's covenant relationship with us. God says, "You will call me my husband" (Hosea 2:16). That's marriage talk. God says of us, "I will betroth you to me *forever*" (Hosea 2:19). Language can't get much stronger than that. Jesus keeps his covenant promise forever. God's unbroken promise to unfaithful people is our example for marriage. His unbreakable promise to us is to shape our unbreakable promise to our spouses. Train your child to enter marriage with the same iron-willed, unwavering promise that Jesus gave to the church: "Never will I leave you or forsake you."

When I teach on this subject, I get questions at this point. Maybe a few have already popped into your head. What about

3. For further study on this topic, I encourage you to read David W. Jones and John K. Tarwater, "Are Biblical Covenants Dissoluble? Toward a Theology of Marriage," *Southwestern Journal of Theology* 47, no. 1 (Fall 2004): 1–11.

abuse? What about adultery? What about addiction? What about abandonment? What if the husband and wife are nothing more than roommates? What if one spouse racks up huge debt without the other's knowledge?

Those are serious issues. I'm not minimizing them. Sin in marriage needs to be addressed head on. Usually both spouses (to some degree) need to be called to repentance and given biblical guidance so that heart and habit changes can occur.

In conservative evangelical circles, the most common interpretation of Scripture is that the Bible makes provision for divorce in the most severe instances: cases of unrepentant sexual unfaithfulness (Matt. 19:9) and abandonment by a gospel-rejecting spouse (1 Cor. 7:15). Whatever your view of the biblical justification for divorce, my hope is that you will champion marriage with your children, even in difficult situations. The end goals, when sin is addressed in marriage, are reconciliation and a renewed marriage centered on Christ.

Why do I say that? How our children respond to sin in their marriages should be patterned after God's response to our sin. Did Jesus leave us when we were unfaithful to him? Did God walk away from us because he grew weary of our addiction? Did God divorce us because we abandoned him for another love? The answer to each of these questions is no. Despite our unfaithfulness, God remains faithful. This certainty lies not in us but in God's covenant commitment. God says he will forgive our sins and remember them no more. Our sin is ugly. It is a stench in God's nose. It grieves God. Yet he did not break his covenant promise.

Marriage Covenants Are Patterned after God's Covenant of Salvation

What makes divorce so horrific in God's eyes is that it involves breaking our covenant with our spouse and thus misrepresents Jesus and his covenant. Jesus keeps his covenant of salvation forever, so this is the example that all married couples are to follow. Jesus never divorces us, so this is the same commitment to which we are to call our children in marriage.

Most people like this idea in theory—until sin enters the picture. Then they often seek biblical justification to end a miserable marriage. But one thing remains: our sin doesn't change God's love. Despite sin, God did not divorce the church.

Take a moment to consider how you have rebelled against God throughout your life—repeatedly, willfully, and habitually. Now consider how God has responded to your sin. In the midst of your rebellion, God sought you out. He offered grace. He invited you back. God's love is unconditional. Hebrews 8:12 sums it up nicely: "I will forgive their wickedness and remember their sins no more." We like hearing those words when they are offered *to* us. It's a whole lot harder when they have to be offered *by* us.

Your child is going to marry someone with warts. No, not a troll—just someone with annoying habits, a strong personality, and a sinful nature. As J. C. Ryle said, marriage is the joining of two sinners, not two saints.[4] This means that marriage preparation must include helping your child to navigate sin in marriage. When two sinners come together, there are bound to be fireworks. What do you do when your spouse sins against you? What happens when the wounding is deep and repetitive? How about when the spouse is unrepentant? Your child may find himself or herself living this reality. What you teach your child today may make the difference between divorce and reconciliation.

Teach your child that he is to do for his future spouse what God has done for him. Teach your child to love as she is loved by God and to forgive as she has been forgiven by Christ. We take our cues on marriage from Christ. We are to forgive our spouses as God has forgiven us (Matt. 6:14–15; Eph. 4:32). We are to bear with the sins of others as God bears with our sin. As much grace as your child has received on the cross, he or she is to give to a future spouse. If your child finds himself or herself in a difficult marriage, this will make the difference between divorce and faithfulness.

4. See J. C. Ryle, *Mark,* Expository Thoughts on the Gospels 1 (Grand Rapids: Baker, 2007), 200.

It is wise to instruct your child how to deal with conflict in a godly manner: to put down his weapons (James 3:5–8), deal with conflict daily (Eph. 4:26), control her words (Eph. 4:29), and forgive freely (Col. 3:13). Otherwise, when there is conflict in marriage, what will your child do? Explode in anger? Give the silent treatment? Withdraw emotionally? Run away? Eventually end the marriage?

As we begin to grasp the depth of God's love for us, that knowledge should affect how we love others—especially a future spouse. God loved us when we were most unlovable. He didn't establish a relationship with us because we were pure or perfect. He doesn't honor his promise of salvation because we are good and godly. God's permanent love for us, despite our ugly adulterous sin, is the same permanent love to which we are to call our children in marriage.

Upholding the Sacredness of Marriage

Divorce is not about one person's relationship with another person. Ultimately, divorce is about a covenant. To reject that covenant is to deface the picture of the gospel that God has embedded in marriage. John Piper writes, "Marriage is not mainly about being or staying in love. It's mainly about telling the truth with our lives. It's about portraying something true about Jesus Christ and the way he relates to his people. It is about showing in real life the glory of the gospel."[5] God's covenant promise of salvation to us is an unconditional, make-it-and-never-break-it promise, and our covenants should be the same.

God's design for marriage is meant to last for life, ending only with the death of a spouse (1 Cor. 7:39). Call your child to a marriage that is for God's glory and your child's good. Boldly proclaim the truth of Scripture to your child and encourage your child to let his or her yes be yes. Provide a grand vision of marriage for your child: *one man and one woman for life.*

5. John Piper, *This Momentary Marriage: A Parable of Permanence* (Wheaton, IL: Crossway, 2012), 26.

Courageous Conversations

1. What is divorce? Do you believe it is ever permissible for a married man and woman to divorce each other?
2. Read Genesis 2:24. What does it mean to "hold fast" to one another?
3. What does Matthew 19:6 suggest about divorce? How should we understand the phrase "let no one separate"?
4. Why does Malachi 2:15 tell a couple not to get divorced?
5. Take a moment and review Malachi 2:14. What is marriage called in this verse?
6. What do James 5:12 and Matthew 5:37 teach us about making and breaking a promise?
7. If marriage is a covenant and is patterned after God's covenant of salvation with us, then what do the following passages teach us?
    a. Psalm 89:34
    b. Hosea 2:16–20 (see esp. v. 19)
    c. Hosea 3:1
8. Take a moment and consider how you have rebelled against God—repeatedly, willfully, and habitually. What does Hebrews 8:12 and 13:5 tell us that God does with our sin?
9. What do the following passages teach us to do with a future spouse who sins against us?
    a. Ephesians 4:32
    b. Matthew 6:14–15
    c. Colossians 3:13
10. When does God permit a marriage to end?
    a. 1 Corinthians 7:39
    b. 1 Corinthians 7:10–16
    c. Mark 10:1–12
    d. Matthew 19:1–10

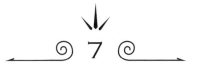

Why Did God Create Marriage?

Three of God's Good Purposes for Marriage

The New Mexico whiptail is an unusual lizard. It grows 7–9 inches long, loves arid places, and is always female. There are no male whiptails. Typically, this would be problematic when it comes to having a baby! But not for the whiptail. The female whiptail can reproduce without the aid of a male.

New Mexico whiptails aren't alone. Some scientists suggest that upward of 5 percent of insects, such as some bees, have this capability—as well as some snails, scorpions, a few fish, and many plants. The technical word for this is the Greek term *parthenogenesis*, which means "virgin creation" or "virgin beginning."

Why didn't God make humans like New Mexico whiptails? If God is capable of creating insects, plants, and animals with the ability to reproduce on their own, it's not a stretch to imagine that he could have done the same with humanity. Instead, God purposefully created humans as man and woman and brought them together in marriage for specific reasons.

As we saw in chapter 4, marriage is *from* God and *for* God. Because God ultimately created marriage to glorify himself, it doesn't exist just for the pleasure of the married couple. A God-honoring marriage exists for a greater purpose. In this chapter, we'll explore three purposes for marriage and explain what God designed marriage to accomplish.

Marriage Is a Picture of the Gospel

Marriage is about love. Only it's not so much about the love of a man for a woman as it is about the love of the Savior for lost sinners. God designed marriage to be a picture that points to a greater reality. *A marriage between one man and one woman isn't the point—it's the pointer.*

What is marriage pointing to? To answer that question, let's look to Ephesians 5:32. In this verse, Paul states that marriage "refers to Christ and the church." Marriage has meaning beyond the love of a man for a woman. It refers to Jesus' sacrificial death on the cross. It refers to God's great love for lost sinners. It refers to redemption in Christ through his shed blood. It refers to sacrifice, service, and submission.

Marriage between a man and a woman is meant to reflect the relationship between Christ and the church. It is a living example of Jesus' love for the church and of the church's submission to Jesus. How Jesus loved the church is how a husband is to love his wife. How the church follows Jesus is how a wife is to follow her husband. Every marriage is a picture that tells the world about Jesus' sacrificial love for us. Marriage points to a greater reality—it's a living, breathing reminder of Calvary.

When I explain this to young people, I tell them that marriage is a lot like a drama or a play. The purpose of a drama is to tell a story. In order for this to happen, actors are given a role in the play. In marriage, the husband is given the Jesus role and the wife is given the church role. The husband is told to live out a Jesus role, which revolves around sacrifice and service for his wife. The wife is to imitate the pattern of the church, which revolves around willingly following her husband's loving leadership.

Paul puts it this way: "Now as the church submits to Christ, so also wives should submit in everything to their husbands. Husbands, love your wives, as Christ loved the church and gave himself up for her" (Eph. 5:24–25). The relationship between a husband and wife points to, and is to be patterned after, what Jesus did for the church and how the church is to respond to Jesus.

Teaching children about marriage is an important element of gospel education. The gospel is the reason that marriage exists. It is embedded in every marriage. Marriage is the silent sermon. It is the living drama. It is a gospel snapshot. It is a gospel show-and-tell. And the world is watching.

Marriage is meant to be seen. Little eyes are watching, and part of what children will believe about marriage has nothing to do with what their parents say and everything to do with how their parents live. Dietrich Bonhoeffer, imprisoned in a Nazi concentration camp, summarized the first purpose of marriage by stating that it comes with "a post of responsibility." That responsibility is to display the gospel for the world and for your children. Bonhoeffer writes,

> Marriage is more than your love for each other. . . . In your love you see only the heaven of your own happiness, but in marriage you are placed at a post of responsibility towards the world and mankind. Your love is your own private possession, but marriage is more than something personal—it is a status, an office. Just as it is the crown, and not merely the will to rule, that makes the king, so it is marriage, and not merely your love for each other, that joins you together in the sight of God and man.[1]

Parent, how clearly is the gospel being displayed through your marriage? If you're a husband, does your child see you loving your wife as Jesus loves the church? If you're a wife, does your child see you submitting to your husband as the church submits to Jesus?

1. Dietrich Bonhoeffer, *Letters and Papers from Prison*, rev. ed. (New York: Touchstone, 1997), 42–43.

Try challenging your child with similar questions. Ask him or her, "When people look at your future marriage, will they see an example of Jesus' love for the church and the church's submission to him?"

Marriage Is the Context for Children

Are you ready to have a fun discussion with your children? Ask them whether they plan to have children and how many they would like to have. When I bring up this topic in premarital counseling, many young couples admit that they haven't given it much thought. If they haven't thought about it, that means that their parents haven't talked about it. That's problematic, because the cultural messages that young people hear on this subject are often anti-children. Let me give you a taste.

Comedian Rita Rudner once said, "My husband and I are either going to buy a dog or have a child. We can't decide to ruin our carpet or ruin our lives." Pets have become replacements for children and have been one reason that the pet market has increased in the United States from 17 billion in 1994 to over 60 billion today.[2] Many young couples are choosing pets in place of children because, as one sarcastic card says, they are "cleaner, cheaper, cuter, easier to train, and don't ruin all my life plans and goals."

Honda CR-V ran a full-page ad containing the question, "Before I have children I want to ____." Under the question are pictures of all kinds of adventures and accomplishments: learning to play the banjo, skydiving, sailing, running a marathon, and climbing the corporate ladder. It encouraged young people to do everything on their to-do list before they took the next step and had children.

The "child-free and loving it" movement suggests that child-lessness is a superior lifestyle choice, and it provides plenty of books to help couples navigate this world. Two examples are *No Kids: 40*

---

2. See "Pet Industry Market Size & Ownership Statistics," American Pet Products Association, accessed June 26, 2017, http://www.AmericanPetProducts.org /press_industrytrends.asp.

Good Reasons NOT to Have Children[3] and *Two is Enough: A Couple's Guide to Living Childless by Choice.*[4] They argue that having children leads to unhappiness, economic challenges, and a decrease in marital satisfaction, and that it lasts for life.

What is the driving motivation behind a movement to discourage parenthood? Selfishness. Having children, the argument goes, will collide with *your* life plan, all the stuff *you* want to do, and *your* happiness. According to this viewpoint, children are a burden, not a blessing.

In their book *Start Your Family*, Candice and Steve Watters make the insightful point that couples weighing the decision to start a family are increasingly surrounded by books, articles, and Web sites spotlighting the costs and sacrifices ahead of them. Those messages encourage couples to think long and hard about the world they'd be bringing children into, and remind them to count all the costs before making such a monumental decision. Caution and preparation are helpful, but sometimes it seems that's all couples can find on the topic of having kids these days. Churches often have little to offer on this subject. Increasingly, it takes vision for "why" to overcome the growing—and often compelling—arguments for "why not."[5]

Candice and Steve apply their observations to the church, and pastors should listen up. But these observations apply to parents as well. Parents and pastors need to talk with young people about this subject and help them embrace a biblical view of childbearing.

Can you provide a compelling biblical vision for your child to combat the arguments for "why not"? Separating marriage from childbearing in discussions is a disservice to young people. Our culture has created an unnatural division between them, but the Bible provides a very different picture. Your child needs a grand,

3. See Corinne Maier, *No Kids: 40 Good Reasons NOT to Have Children* (repr., Toronto, Ontario: Emblem Editions, 2009).

4. See Laura S. Scott, *Two Is Enough: A Couple's Guide to Living Childless by Choice* (Berkeley, CA: Seal Press, 2009).

5. See Steve and Candice Watters, *Start Your Family: Inspiration for Having Babies* (Chicago: Moody Publishers, 2009), 27, 29.

Jesus-centered, countercultural vision for why they should have children.

I summarize the biblical vs. the cultural message in the following way: *early, often, and many* instead of *late, long, and few*. American culture tells young people to delay having children until later in life, wait longer between having children, and have only one or two total. The unwritten rule is that you can have a third child if the first two were the same gender and you want to try for a child of the opposite gender. If you have four children, people will remind you that there are ways to prevent this from happening. Have five or more children, and welcome to the freak show.

Why have children? First, God commands married couples to have children. In Genesis 1:28 we are told, "God blessed [Adam and Eve]. And God said to them, 'Be fruitful and multiply and fill the earth and subdue it.'" This is the first command that God gives to humans, and it comes right on the heels of marriage. God blessed Adam and Eve's marriage and then told them to work and have babies so that they could be good stewards of God's creation. Because of the biblical command, it should not be a matter of *whether* your child will have kids when he or she is married but *how many* he or she will have.

How many children should you encourage your child to have? The Bible never gives a number, so I won't either. There are small families and large families in the Bible: families with one child and families the size of a small orphanage. Roy Zuck claims that the average number of children per monogamous couple in the Bible is 6.1.[6] That doesn't mean that we need to aim for that number. But the pattern of Scripture is helpful to recognize. The Bible is always pro-children, and you and your child should be pro-children, too. I've had countless older couples tell me, "We wish we had more children," but I've never had parents tell me that they wish they had one fewer (even though we've all had our moments).

6. See Roy B. Zuck, *Precious in His Sight: Childhood and Children in the Bible* (Grand Rapids: Baker Books, 1996), 92.

Because God is pro-children, this should inform our decision-making. As you talk to your child, teach him or her the "round up" principle. When deciding between a certain number of children to have, round up to the higher number. One child or two? Round up to two. Two or three children? Round up to three. Three or four children? Round up to four. You get the point. When culture says, "Late, long, and few," the Bible says, "Early, often, and many."

Second, the Bible speaks of having children as desirable. Having many children is viewed as a blessing from God, while barrenness is painful.[7] A full quiver (many children) is described as a good thing (Ps. 127:5). Leah's response at the birth of her son reflects the Bible's overall demeanor toward children: "Leah said, 'Happy am I!'" (Gen. 30:13). In the Bible, women of faith pursue childbirth, as it is motherhood that makes the world's salvation possible through the birth of Jesus (1 Tim. 2:15). In addition, children are the Bible's retirement plan (1 Tim. 5:8) and help us to understand the father heart of God.

One author notes, "The kingdom of God looks like a busy cul-de-sac filled with playful children, not an intimate table for two. As Zechariah 8:5 puts it, 'the streets of [Zion] shall be full of boys and girls playing in its streets.'"[8] If the kingdom of God is filled with children, doesn't it make sense for your child's home to be filled with them as well?

Third, having children is a means to grow our own faith in God. Parenthood causes us to be in the very place where God wants us—in a state of total dependence on him. Remember all the "what ifs" that run through a person's head at times like this? *What if I can't afford another child? What if I don't have enough love or time for another child? What if the child has a disability or is difficult to parent? What if my child grows up to love the Green Bay Packers?* (Agreed—that would be

7. Just look to Hannah (see 1 Sam. 1), Abraham and Sarah (see Gen. 16), Tamar (see Gen. 38), and Elizabeth (see Luke 1:7).

8. David Schrock, "Children: A Blessed Necessity for Christian Marriages," *The Journal of Discipleship and Family Ministry* 4, no. 1 (Fall–Winter 2013), 64.

horrible.) Your child may head toward the late, long, and few route as the "what ifs" become convincing. If this is your child's path, then this is where you must nudge him or her to trust God and depend on him to provide for future needs.

To "be fruitful and multiply" is one of the purposes of marriage. In God's plan, children are brought into the world through marriage, which is meant to serve as the primary evangelism and discipleship center for children. In the Bible, marriage and childbearing are so closely connected that one could argue that, if a young person is not ready to have children, then he or she is not ready for marriage. A childless or child-lite marriage deviates from God's expected norm and ought not to be purposefully pursued.

Pro-children. This is what I see in Scripture and what I encourage you to impress on your child.

Marriage Provides Companionship

Marriage fulfills the basic needs that human beings have. This includes physical intimacy (1 Cor. 7:1–5) as well as companionship (Prov. 2:17). Malachi 2:14 says, "She is your companion." We don't use the term *companionship* much today, unless you are talking about a dog, so it is necessary to help young people understand that this is the Bible's way of talking about deep, sacrificial friendship.

One of the best things that we can do to prepare our children for marriage is to teach them how to develop and maintain friendships. Countless marriages struggle because the couple does not know how to handle anger, communicate with each other, or forgive each other when hurt. Sadly, plenty of married couples trade being best friends for being roommates. The relational principles that our children learn in friendships today can be applied to marriage tomorrow. If parents are intentional, the relationships that our children have with family and friends can become a rich training ground for marriage.

What is at the heart of Christ-centered relationships? I believe Paul answers that question in Philippians 2 when he says, "Jesus made himself nothing, taking the form of a servant . . . [and died] on a cross" (Phil. 2:7–8). Like Jesus, "Let each of you look not only to his own interests, but also to the interests of others" (Phil. 2:4). Our children are to imitate the others-centered mind-set of Jesus rather than to pursue their own happiness at the expense of others. Every child should memorize Philippians 2:4. Plaster it all over your home. Repeat it often.

The problem that chokes the life out of countless marriages is almost always selfishness. One person pursues his or her own desires without care or consideration for the other person. Here's where this intersects with children: Children do not suddenly become selfish as adults. Children carry into marriage the habits and perspectives they developed when they were younger. Selfish children become selfish adults. This means that one of the best gifts you can give to your child's future marriage is to train him or her to be radically concerned with the needs of others. Parents who give in to the desires and demands of a child not only will have their hands full as the child ages but are raising an adult who will expect a marriage to revolve around him or her.

Your goal as a parent is to *train your child to be others-centered, not me-centered.* Will your child serve others in the family even when it is costly? Will your child sacrifice something that he or she wants because it will make a sibling happy? Or will your child demand what he or she wants and scream, fight, hit, argue, or give the silent treatment?

Think about the last time things got ugly because your child didn't get what he or she wanted. How often does this happen? How do you respond when it does? Imagine what a future marriage will look like if this child's heart and habits are not changed.

Parents who allow their children to grow up with a me-centered rather than an others-centered mind-set are setting their children up to fail in every meaningful relationship they will ever have. Selfish individuals are those who act as if they have little responsibility to others, feel limited obligation to care for others' needs, resent others infringing on their priceless personal space, and are blind to what is happening in the lives of others.

Children must be trained to look to the interests of others because they are born caring only for themselves. Looking to the interests of others comes only through a changed heart and controlled habits. As you prepare your child for marriage, be sure to teach him or her these three key relational skills:

- willingness to forgive
- ability to control anger
- skill to carry a conversation

You will be able to explore each of these areas in greater depth in the study section.

Courageous Conversations

1. The Bible teaches us that God created marriage for a purpose. Why do you think God created marriage?
2. According to the following passages, why did God create marriage?
    a. Ephesians 5:22–33 (see esp. v. 32)
    b. Genesis 1:28
    c. Proverbs 2:17 and Malachi 2:14
3. What does Paul compare marriage to in Ephesians 5:24–25?
4. What does it mean that marriage is a picture of the gospel? In what ways can a marriage be a good example of the gospel or a bad example of the gospel to others?
5. When you get married someday, would you like to have children? If so, how many?
6. What do the following passages teach us about having children?
    a. Psalm 127:5
    b. Genesis 30:13
    c. Luke 1:13
7. Read Philippians 2:4 and discuss ways in which husbands and wives can look to the interests of their spouses. Even though you are not married, what are ways that you can look to the interests of others in your life right now?

8. Discuss key relational skills that your child can develop today that will help him or her in marriage tomorrow.
   a. Ephesians 4:26
   b. Ephesians 4:29
   c. Colossians 3:13
   d. Colossians 3:17
   e. James 1:19–20

PREPARING YOUR
SON FOR MARRIAGE

Embracing His Role as Husband

In the last chapter, we saw that the relationship between a man and a woman in marriage should point toward the relationship between Jesus and the church. This means that while teaching children the biblical definition of marriage is a good start, more is needed. Children need to be taught the roles of a husband and a wife in marriage. If not, they may end up like Matt and Mandy.

Matt and Mandy sat in my office in complete silence. When I walked in, I could feel the ice-cold tension between them. Their marriage was relatively young—only five years old. Yet it had struggled for years. When I asked what they thought was at the root of their problems, Mandy suggested communication problems but couldn't explain why. Matt said nothing.

When I asked what they had done about it, Mandy mentioned that they had seen multiple counselors but nothing had helped. Again Matt said nothing. At least this time he nodded in agreement. As I probed further, Mandy did most of the talking and Matt did most of the nodding. Mandy pointed out that what was happening in my office was what happened daily in their home. She blamed Matt for poor communication and for withdrawing from her emotionally. Of course, Matt nodded. But this time he also said something insightful: "It feels like our marriage is out of sync."

Out of sync. That summarizes the experience that many have in marriage when they do not understand the biblical roles of husband and wife. Matt and Mandy's problem was not primarily a communication problem but a role problem. For Matt and Mandy, being out of sync relationally was connected to being out of step biblically. Matt had not learned how to lead, and Mandy did not know how to follow, and their communication suffered as a result.

Once Matt and Mandy learned the biblical roles of a husband and a wife and applied this teaching to their marriage, their relationship began to steadily improve. After a few meetings, Matt said something that I hear often from couples whom I counsel: "I wish I had known this sooner. It has changed our marriage."

The Biblical Role of a Husband and a Wife

During premarital counseling, I ask couples, "Did your parents ever talk with you about the role of a husband and a wife in marriage?" Most say no. It's not a subject that most parents are talking about with their children. It needs to be. Here's why.

Every marriage exists to point to the gospel, and this happens as a husband and wife operate in the roles that God has designed. When married couples do not live in a God-designed manner, it can present a distorted picture of the gospel to others, which results in a poor witness for Christ. If we want our children's marriages to communicate the God-intended message of the truth of the gospel, then we must ensure that they understand the role God has given to them in order to accomplish that outcome.

Teaching your child his or her role in marriage will help your child to establish a healthy and happy marriage that honors Christ. When couples do not live according to God's design for marriage, it can result in a dysfunctional marriage relationship. Parents, you are giving your child an incredible gift when you help him or her to live according to God's ways in marriage. Neither marriage nor any other area of life ever goes well if we try to do things our way rather than God's way.

Out of necessity, every husband and wife split up the responsibilities of their marriage in some way. The question is, how is this determined? How does a couple decide who leads the family, manages the home, earns money, or raises children? Who does the countless daily tasks that arise, such as yard work, laundry, cooking, financial management, and overseeing the spiritual climate of the home? Someone has to do these things. Again, how is this determined? Whose role is it to lead when there is a stalemate in conflict management, communication, and physical intimacy? Is this left up to every couple to determine on their own, or did God communicate the roles of a husband and a wife in marriage? These are important questions, and every child should know the answers.

As we've seen, God created and designed marriage. It makes sense, then, that he would also define the role of a husband and a wife in marriage. God wouldn't design the whole (the marriage) without designing the parts of the whole (the roles). Marriage works best when its parts operate as they were designed to.

In order to accomplish this, God gives both husbands and wives a detailed job description. In the Bible he clearly communicates the essential duties and expectations of each of their roles. Job descriptions are a helpful thing. They tell us what to do and what not to do. Job descriptions inform us how to use our time and what our priorities should be. They tell us what our responsibility is and what we will be held accountable for. God has done that for the husband and the wife.

What do you believe are a man's and woman's roles in marriage? Can you summarize each of their job descriptions in a sentence or, better yet, a word? Can you point me to where that comes from in Scripture and then clearly explain that role to your child? You may want to write your description in the margin of this book right now and compare it to what will be presented in this chapter and the chapter following.

PREPARING YOUR SON FOR MARRIAGE

With children, it's helpful to be as concise and clear as possible. This allows you to be extremely focused when you explain and train. The Bible summarizes the role of a husband and a wife in one word each: *head* and *helper*. These words are found in Genesis 2:15–18 and Ephesians 5:22–33 and form the backbone for the roles of a husband and a wife.

If you do not have a son, I encourage you to read this chapter anyway, as it is essential that your daughter understand her future husband's role in marriage. Your daughter will use the information in this chapter as criteria to help her choose whom to date and eventually marry. We will explore the role of a wife in the next chapter.

The Husband Is the Head

According to the Bible, the role of the husband can be summarized in one word: *head*. The word comes from Ephesians 5:23, where Paul states, "For the husband is the head of the wife even as Christ is the head of the church his body, and is himself its Savior." I like to use biblical words with the children I teach, but I always explain what they mean. In a nutshell, headship means loving leadership and sacrificial service. Headship is patterned after Jesus' love for the church, which means that a husband is called to be a servant leader, to protect, and to provide.

Future husbands should be trained to continually ask, "How can I serve you?" as this question summarizes the role that God has given men in marriage.

Some people will argue that the husband's role as head and the wife's role as helper are a cultural expression of the first century and no longer apply today. They suggest that, because the culture has changed, the roles of husband and wife have changed. Thus, as the argument goes, the traditional idea of the man as the leader of the home is the skeletal remains of a first-century idea. The problem with this argument is that the roles of husband and wife were introduced at creation, not in the first century. What Paul says in Ephesians 5:22–33 is an extension of what Moses records in Genesis 2:15–18.

106

Ephesians 5:22–33 gives Genesis 2:15–18's greater meaning. The difference is Christ. He is the model to help us to properly apply headship.

Encourage your son to look to Christ, in order to understand his role in marriage, and to imitate Christ as a servant leader who is benevolent to his family and is busy protecting and providing for the people over whom God has given him spiritual responsibility.

To Be a Servant Leader

If we want to teach our boys to be godly husbands, then we need to encourage them to look to Christ. Paul says it like this: "Husbands, love your wives, as Christ loved the church and gave himself up for her" (Eph. 5:25). What does this mean?

This means that a husband's leadership is about giving, not receiving. The husband's role comes with a towel and a washbasin, not a throne and a crown. The leadership that Jesus models is characterized by love and oriented toward giving, so your son must learn to pattern his leadership after what Jesus did on the cross and to do for his family what Jesus did for the church. That is headship. And when it is properly applied, I've never met a woman who does not desire this in a husband.

How did Jesus love the church? He focused on others rather than on himself. He came to serve, not to be served. He used his authority on behalf of others, not to benefit himself. He gave his life away so that our broken relationship with the Father could be restored. Jesus shows us that being the head is costly. Your son needs to learn this truth. He needs to enter marriage recognizing that true headship is not selfish; rather, it is self-giving. When the husband makes Christ's love for the church the pattern for loving his wife, his love will manifest itself through regular times of sacrifice and a habit of service for his wife.

The kind of headship described in the Bible is gentle, caring, and others-focused. By design, a husband's role is to be concerned with the needs and feelings of others. If he does not show that concern, he will often misuse or abuse the role. If you have experienced poor leadership in the home, my hope is that your experience does not lead to a rejection of what the Bible teaches. When a husband is harsh, controlling, or absent, this isn't biblical headship. It's ugly and unfortunate. When a husband leads well, biblical headship is attractive and desirable.

Boys need to be trained to think of others, care for others, and sacrifice for others, because this is not their natural tendency. Men, as well as boys, have the tendency to be rough and gruff with words and deeds, which is why Paul reminds fathers to pay attention to how they treat members of their families (Eph. 6:4).

One of the best ways you can prepare your son to be a good husband is to teach him to serve his siblings and mother and father. If he does not learn how to do it now, why should he do it later? I encourage you to use the mundane, everyday experiences in order to train your son to serve others. You can do this by defining acts of service to others as forms of leadership and then affirming your son when he serves others. This is marriage training, and your son's future wife will thank you for it! A servant-minded, self-giving love is central to a husband's role in the home and naturally leads to the next two roles that the Bible gives husbands.

To Provide

The husband's role also includes provision for his family. Genesis 2:15 tells us, "The Lord God took the man and put him in the garden of Eden to work it." By working in the garden, Adam would provide for himself and his family.

Work is central to the role of a husband. A godly husband works hard to take care of his family. Thus, boys need to be taught to work hard and to do hard work. The Bible never speaks of idleness as a positive trait. Lazy husbands do not make good husbands, so put your son to work in a way that serves your family and blesses others. After all, God did the same for Adam. He placed him in a garden and put him to work.

At the Mulvihill home, we have a garden, chickens, and a dog, because they are tools that teach boys to work and, as a result, to learn to be future husbands who know how to provide for their families. Give your son work that will stretch him and teach responsibility. Invite him to work alongside you and to learn from your example. Teach your son to sweat for the glory of God in service to his family by working hard.

The ability to work and financially support a family is important, but it is only part of what it means to provide. God also expects husbands to provide for their families spiritually. In Ephesians, Paul tells husbands to love their wives in a way that encourages them to grow spiritually and become more like Jesus (Eph. 5:26). Paul uses the word *sanctification*, which means to be set apart for God. The husband is to encourage all members of the family to obey God, follow Christ, and say no to sin. Teach your son that a godly husband is to be concerned with his family's *holiness*, which leads to their *happiness*.

Plenty of husbands work hard to provide every possible comfort and enjoyment for their family but do not set a spiritual tone for a home that encourages every member to passionately pursue Christ. By worldly standards they are rich, but by God's standards they are spiritually bankrupt. Your son needs to have the strong conviction that what matters in eternity isn't the fact that he provided a big house, a luxury car, a good education, or a fun family vacation for his future wife and children. Paul tells husbands to aim for something much greater than square footage and weeks on the beach. Husbands are to provide for their families by being the spiritual leader. They are to lead in a way that encourages their families to treasure Christ and stand before the Lord without spot or blemish.

How do you do that with grade school or teenage boys? By modeling this kind of leadership. Boys learn to become men of God by imitating other godly men. Encourage your son to watch, listen, learn, and imitate. My father read and discussed the Word of God with our family for my entire childhood, and now I do the same with my family. I learned by watching him. Your son will learn by watching you. He will learn that the Word of God should be central in the home and that fathers need to take the lead spiritually. He will learn how to provide a rich feast of God's Word for his family. What you are doing for him, in family worship, he will need to do for his family. How will your son learn to be the spiritual leader of his home if you do not show him?

If you are a single mother, you should step into the spiritual leadership role in the home and encourage your son to imitate your example with his future family. A grandfather, uncle, or godly man can be invited to step intentionally into a surrogate role in order to teach a boy what it means to be a biblical man. The biblical example we are given is that of Timothy, whose mother, grandmother, and Paul all invested in his growing into a godly man.

But how will your son *truly* know how to lead his family in the worship of God? By practicing! Give your son occasional, regular opportunities to lead the family in prayer, Bible reading, and the praise of God. Jen and I regularly give our sons the opportunity to lead the family in worship. At times, I have them read aloud from the Bible. Other times, they lead the family discussion. I want my sons to be comfortable in this role. As they say, practice makes perfect. The same concept can be applied to teaching our sons to be spiritual leaders of their homes.[1] In order to be good spiritual leaders, sons need to be taught how to lead family worship. Boys need to learn how to open the Bible, read it, discuss it, explain it, and apply it to their families.

We are comfortable training our sons to hit a baseball and drive a car, but many parents have never considered the importance of training their sons to be the spiritual leaders of the home. We would never

---

1. If you are looking for devotional books to use with your family, my favorites include Marty Machowski, *Long Story Short* (Greensboro, NC: New Growth Press, 2010); Marty Machowski, *Old Story New* (Greensboro, NC: New Growth Press, 2012); John B. Leuzarder, *The Gospel for Children* (Wapwallopen, PA: Shepherd Press, 2002); and Carine MacKenzie, *My First Book of Questions and Answers* (Fearn, Ross-shire, UK: Christian Focus, 2011). Each of these books contains short questions and answers and is perfect for use with grade-school children. For older children, books such as Peter Jeffery, *Bitesize Theology* (Grand Rapids: Evangelical Press, 2000) and R.C. Sproul, *Essential Truths of the Christian Faith* (Carol Stream, IL: Tyndale, 1992) are excellent helps.

hand our children the keys to the car without instruction and practice. Most would agree that spiritual leadership is far more important than proficiency at baseball, yet many parents spend a disproportionate amount of time training children in areas that matter far less. Tell your son that he is preparing today to be the future spiritual leader of his home. This is a large, compelling vision. On the day your son is married, the spiritual leadership component of his role should be second nature because he has had plenty of practice at home.

To Protect

But there is more to Genesis 2:15. Not only was Adam told to provide for his family, he was also told to protect his family: "The LORD God took the man and put him in the garden of Eden to work it *and keep it.*" The word *keep* refers to protecting that which God had entrusted to the man's care. God's command to "keep" is his call to husbands to defend their families from harm and evil.

This is precisely what Adam did not do in Genesis 3. God had just told Adam that his job was to provide for Eve and protect her. Then came the test. Satan, in the form of a serpent, approached Eve and tempted her to do what God had forbidden. Genesis 3:6 tells us that Adam "was with her." He was there. If ever there were a time for Adam to defend his wife, this was it! But what did Adam do? He did what countless men do today: he stood there. He did nothing to protect his wife. He was spiritually ambivalent even though he was physically present. He knew that the serpent was encouraging Eve to do what God had commanded them not to. He saw her take the fruit. Yet he did nothing. Like a true gentleman, Adam let Eve go first. Then he followed his wife and plunged headlong into spiritual death by eating the fruit.

Genesis 3:6 is a case study of what *not* to do as a husband. Rather than protect, Adam permitted. Rather than keep sin out, he let it in. This is a great verse to read and discuss with your son in order to show him that there are major consequences for families when husbands don't lead. Ask your son to imagine what might happen in his family if he does not lead. We want our sons to feel the weight of negative consequences that await their families if they do not do what God has asked of them. This method of instruction follows the pattern of Proverbs, in which a scenario is presented and the son is warned to avoid a certain path in life.

Your job is to help your son understand the seriousness of the role that God has given him. You should give him a God-sized vision to be a watchful warrior over his family and to slay any dragons that come his way. This was the role that God gave Adam. Adam was Eve's knight, purposed with protecting her. What Adam could not accomplish, Jesus did. The serpent in Genesis is the dragon of Revelation. The redemption story of Scripture culminates with Jesus, the Warrior King, slaying the dragon and fully conquering sin, Satan, and death (Revelation 20:2–3). That makes Jesus a dragon slayer. Move over, meek and mild Jesus. Hello, Warrior King.

Husbands are called to imitate Christ, the dragon slayer and the Lamb who was slain. Boys need this double vision. One without the other is incomplete. A godly man is willing to lay down his life for others, just as Jesus did. He will do this every day through loving service to his family, but he may someday be called to do that more dramatically. When there is a loud noise in the middle of the night in the other room, the husband does not send his wife armed with a baseball bat to investigate. In the face of danger, he is called to the front lines, not the foxhole. If needed, like Christ did, husbands are called to sacrifice their lives in order to serve and protect their families. Remind your son that a self-giving love is central to a man's role in life. To lead may mean to bleed. Drill it into your son that leadership is costly. Jesus came to serve and gave his life as a ransom for many. He is calling your son to do the same.

Your son needs to be given a biblical vision to be both a physical protector and a spiritual protector for his future family. The husband's role comes not only with a towel and a washbasin but also with a sword and a shield. Call your son to be a warrior and to slay dragons. Watch his eyes light up. Watch him rise to the challenge. God created guys to fight for their ladies and to willingly place themselves in front of danger. Don't believe me? Ask any guy if he has ever dreamed about rescuing the damsel in distress. If he's honest, he'll tell you that he has. God has hardwired men to be watchful warriors.

Husbands need to be skillful with both the sword and the shield. They need to work diligently to shield their families from harmful ideas and influences that seek to take them captive (Col. 2:8). What would this include? Threats could come from media, educational teachings, corrupting friendships, and false worldviews, to name a few. Each has the potential to influence young people to reject Christ and pursue sin. Your son must learn to be a watchful warrior over the hearts of those in his care. Far too many husbands are ambivalent regarding what their families are watching, who they spend time with, and what they believe. A husband is to be vigilant to see that every member of his family loves the Lord with his or her whole heart and to work to remove any idols that have captivated the minds of his family members.

In a better world, a husband would need only a shield. Unfortunately that is not the world we live in. Sin and Satan are alive and well. Sin is knocking at our door, and Satan seeks to devour our families. Husbands are to fight the good fight of faith, not only for themselves but also for their wives, children, and grandchildren. That means that young boys need to be trained to use the sword. Teach your son to be brave, to stand in the gap, and to fight for his family if need be. Most likely this will be on the spiritual front and will manifest itself in prayer and the reading of God's Word—the most powerful swords a husband can wield. However, it's also possible that your son will need to physically protect his family. Is your son prepared on this front?

A great way to teach boys to be protectors and providers is to give them toy swords and guns. As a son grows older, he can graduate to a pocketknife, a hatchet, snares, and a BB gun—and, if he is trustworthy and responsible, a low-caliber rifle to be used on hunts with Dad or Grandpa. I want to encourage you to be intentional with the toys and gifts that you give your son.

With a little thought, you can use the everyday toys that your son plays with to give him a vision to be the provider for and protector of his future family. I take my sons hunting and fishing. We build forts. We have lightsaber duels and cowboy adventures. Backyards, lakes, and woods are the perfect classrooms for teaching boys to be protectors and providers. While we're having our fun, we talk about what it means to be the protector and provider of a family and how God gave us tools, such as knives and guns, to do that. I love seeing my boys glow with pride as they hold a stringer of fish or help cook a pheasant dinner and state that they are providing for their family. Used with proper training and for the right purpose, swords and guns are valuable and redemptive. They should be on the top of your list when it comes to marriage training for your son. My classroom is the outdoors; maybe yours is the garage or the living room. A hammer and saw, a lawn mower, a ratchet set, or any number of other items can accomplish the same outcome.

What Headship Is Not

You may reject the traditional role of a man as the head of the home. If you do, my guess is that you aren't rejecting an ideology as much as you are rejecting an experience. It is not uncommon to hear about a husband who is dictatorial, harsh, and self-focused. If this has been your experience, I can understand why you may have strong feelings against the idea of male headship. But, to be clear, this sort of behavior is not what the Bible teaches nor what I am advocating.

Any exercise of headship that is not benevolent and loving is a sinful expression of this leadership role. It doesn't mean that what the Bible says about a husband's role is false or is an outdated idea. It means that sometimes men are bad husbands. What they do doesn't align with who God calls them to be. There is a distinction to be made between the role that God calls husbands to and their implementation of that role. Unbiblical implementation must be rejected, not the role itself. Some teachers are harsh, but that doesn't mean we should do away with all teachers. Some countries have dictatorial rulers, but that doesn't mean they should eliminate government.

Teachers and governments aren't the problem. Neither is

headship. The problem is poor implementation. With that in mind, let's look at three things that headship is not.

Headship Is Not Dictatorship

Headship does not mean that a husband has totalitarian control and barks out orders like a military general for his family to follow. Unfortunately, some husbands operate in this mode. They lead with a heavy hand. It's their way or the highway. They call the shots. They are the decision makers on all matters big and small, and they leave little room for discussion. It's very one-sided. Maybe you've experienced this form of leadership, but it isn't biblical headship. While such a man's intentions may be good, his implementation is not.

Headship Is Not Harsh

Headship does not give husbands the freedom to say or do whatever they want. Nor is it an excuse to yell or operate in anger. In fact, husbands who take their role seriously take Ephesians 4:29 seriously: "Let no corrupting talk come out of your mouths, but only such as is good for building up, as fits the occasion, that it may give grace to those who hear." The husband is to be concerned with the feelings and needs of others. Mistreating anyone in the name of leadership does not please the Lord and is the opposite of what the Bible expects of the husband.

Headship Is Not Superiority

Headship does not mean that women are inferior to men. The husband and wife have the same value but different roles. Equality in value does not necessitate sameness in role. Which is more valuable, a fork or a spoon? A key or the lock? A boat or its motor? In each of these examples, the items are equal in value but different in role. This does not make one item superior and one inferior. It makes them different. Unfortunately, some husbands don't understand this. They equate difference in role with difference in value. That is a mistake, and it is not what the Bible teaches.

When explaining this to your child, tell your son that the Bible doesn't give husbands the freedom to be controlling or mean or to act as if they are worth more than their wives. These are all poor implementations of headship.

Becoming a Godly Husband

One of my favorite manhood verses in the Bible is nestled in the middle of a long list of genealogies. If you read too fast, you'll miss it. In 1 Chronicles 7:40, the author pauses to describe the men of the tribe of Asher. He rarely adds commentary for the other twelve tribes, so this tells me that there was something special about these men: "All these were descendants of Asher—heads of families, choice men, brave warriors and outstanding leaders."

Jen and I named one of our sons Asher, because we want 1 Chronicles 7:40 to be his vision for manhood. In my opinion, this passage is one of the best summaries of manhood in Scripture. Reread the passage's description of an exemplary man: He is the head of his family. A choice man. A brave warrior. An outstanding leader. And he is ready for battle. The men of Asher were the heads of their homes. They had godly character. And they were trained to be brave warriors who were ready for battle.

Will that be your son? Prepare your son to be the head of his home, a man of godly character, a sacrificial leader, and a brave warrior, and he is on the right path to being a great husband. Focus on teaching your son to be the head by leading, protecting, and providing. Doing so will decrease the likelihood that your son will end up in a marriage that is out of sync, and it will help him to become a husband who honors Christ.

Courageous Conversations

1. What one word does Ephesians 5:23 use to summarize the role of a husband? What does it mean to be the head of a marriage?
2. What example should a husband keep in mind as he operates as a servant leader to his wife? Read Ephesians 5:23.

3. Ask your son to assess himself as a servant leader to others. How is he doing as a self-giving, servant-minded family member and friend to others?

4. Study Ephesians 5:25–26. In what two ways did Jesus love the church? How do these two responsibilities apply to a husband's love for his wife?

5. What two roles does Genesis 2:15 give to a husband? When the Bible says "work it" and "keep it," what does that mean? How do these two roles apply to a man's role as the husband?

6. What are ways that a husband is to provide for his family? Read the following passages:
   a. 1 Thessalonians 4:11–12
   b. Ephesians 5:26; 6:4
   c. Proverbs 6:6–8

7. What four things does 1 Chronicles 7:40 teach about being a biblical man? How can these help a man to be a good husband?

8. According to Ephesians 6:4 and 1 Peter 3:7, a husband is not operating in a loving manner if he does what kinds of things?

9. Ask your child to summarize the role of a husband in one sentence.

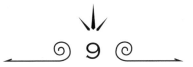

Preparing Your Daughter for Marriage

Embracing Her Role as Wife

When I asked my soon-to-be–four-year-old daughter what she wanted for her birthday, she said, "A princess dress with a fairy wand and a Cinderella doll with a carriage." So I did what every great dad does and went to the Internet to see what I could find. My search brought me to the Barbie website, and I decided to see what they had available.

On the "career page," I found all kinds of different working-women Barbies. There was doctor Barbie, art teacher Barbie, baker Barbie, rock star Barbie, veterinarian Barbie, architect Barbie, and even professional snowboarder Barbie. Noticeably absent was Barbie as a wife or mother. I'm not arguing against women having jobs outside the house. I'm recognizing a subtle message being given to girls that an ambition for marriage or motherhood is a lesser ambition than being a doctor or teacher. That is an unfortunate message. While society may undervalue a woman's role in marriage, God does not. In a day and age when a second income is encouraged and career accomplishments are affirmed, young girls need to learn that the role of a wife is far more precious than jewels and that the works of a wife are praiseworthy (Prov. 31:10; 31). In light of eternity, a woman's work at home is worth more than the largest sum of money and is worthy of great honor.

Girls hear from the world that a role centered on the home is not valuable or desirable. Nothing could be further from the truth. Women are created with a God-ordained role that is not interchangeable with any other member of the family. It's a valuable role and one for you to help your daughter understand.

Let's explore the role that God has given wives.

The Wife Is the Helper

According to the Bible, the role of the wife can be summarized in one word: *helpmate*. The word comes from Genesis 2:18, where God says, "It is not good that man should be alone; I will make him a helper fit for him." The Hebrew word for *helper* carries with it the idea of providing strength and support in an area that another lacks. God created a wife to come alongside her husband in order to offer support and supply strength where it is needed. This is a high and holy task. Eve was created as Adam's helpmate, and together they formed a perfect team using their complementary roles to accomplish the work given to them by God.

To be a *helpmate* means to lovingly follow and faithfully support. Women, whether single or married, can fulfill this role as they assist others who need help. A wife in particular is called to be a willing follower, to manage her home, and to raise children to love Jesus. Your daughter needs to learn how to support her husband and manage the affairs of her home.

God has designed women to be helpers in many different ways, which includes emotional, physical, and spiritual help for their husbands. Lizz Wann states, "God is calling us to be a helper like he is a helper. If God himself is a helper, then we know what he has called us to is something founded in power and strength."[1] John 14:26

---

1. Liz Wann, "At Home and at War: How a Woman Fights for Her Man,"

describes God's role as a helper: "The Helper, the Holy Spirit, whom the Father will send in my name, he will teach you all things and bring to your remembrance all that I have said to you." Encourage your daughter to look to God in order to understand her role in marriage and to be a helper like he is a helper.

Future wives should be trained to continually ask, "How can I help you?" as this question summarizes the role that God has given women in marriage.

To Be a Willing Follower

Authority is a funny thing. People want to be *in authority* but not *under authority*. People want to be in charge and in control. We would rather tell someone what to do than be told what to do. Today, girls are hearing that it's better to lead than to follow. Biblically, this is not the case. God gives the roles of leading and following for the sake of serving him and advancing his kingdom. Each provides a unique value and critical function that cannot be replicated or replaced by the other.

We have already seen that God commands husbands to be servant leaders. When it comes to wives, God commands that they be willing followers. Being a willing follower is the one command that is repeatedly given to wives in Scripture. Here are three examples:

Wives, be subject to your own husbands. (1 Peter 3:1)

Wives, submit to your husbands, as is fitting in the Lord. (Col. 3:18)

Wives, submit to your own husbands, as to the Lord (Eph. 5:22).

Submission is not a popular word in our society today. It carries a lot of baggage, but it is important for us to be able to explain. I use the phrase *willing follower* to do this, since that that easier for a child

Desiring God, January 18, 2017, http://www.desiringgod.org/articles/at-home -and-at-war.

to understand. To *submit* means to come under the leadership of another. A wife honors her husband, and the Lord, when she yields to his leadership and defers to his authority. Her disposition is to be one that seeks to affirm his leadership, agree with him when possible, and assist him according to her gifting. Proverbs 31:12 says that such a woman "does him good, not harm, all the days of her life." This is to be the general demeanor of a wife.

In Titus 2:3–5, mothers and grandmothers are commanded to teach the next generation of wives their God-designed role in marriage: "Older women . . . train the young women to love their husbands and children . . . and [be] submissive to their own husbands." If God specifically tells moms to teach something to their daughters, then it is important!

Being a willing follower is the first and most important role for your daughter to learn when it comes to marriage. She must learn what it means to come under authority and to willingly follow the lead of another. This is so important that it is not a learn-it-on-the-job kind of teaching. Train your daughter from her earliest days to willingly follow the authorities whom God has placed in her life. If she learns to follow authority in general, then she will have the tools she needs to apply these same principles to her future marriage. A daughter who willingly follows a father's leadership will likely do the same for a husband. One is a training ground for the other.

This doesn't mean you should raise a wimpy doormat. It means you should focus on her heart. Pay attention to your daughter's independent, argumentative, and stubborn behavior, as these actions reveal a heart that is not willing to follow authority. To be a godly helper, your daughter must learn to have a cooperative spirit and an agreeable attitude (Prov. 31:26, 28). These internal qualities result in a gentle demeanor that is beautiful (1 Peter 3:1–6).

A wife who is unwilling to be under the authority of her husband creates an out-of-sync, emotionally draining, combative relationship that will erode in intimacy over time. There cannot be two heads in marriage. I like to joke that anything with two heads belongs in the circus. This may seem funny on a page, but it's not humorous when observed in real life. If roles are reversed and a wife steps into the overall leadership role of the home, the husband will often withdraw or fight. It is worth noting that the Bible never refers to the wife as the head or the husband as a helpmate. The role of helpmate is reserved for women. Only Eve was a suitable helper for Adam (Gen. 2:18; 20).

In Scripture, a husband is called to sacrifice and a wife is called to surrender. Both are called to difficult tasks. A husband who serves his wife makes the wife's job of surrendering much easier. Submission is not for a husband to demand but for a wife to give. This is where willingness comes into play. A wife must freely choose to come under the leadership of her husband.

What does this look like in everyday life? In marriage it means that the husband sets the direction (loving Jesus and living for him) and creates an atmosphere (loving one another), and a wife helps to implement this in the home. It does not mean that a wife cannot have her own opinion or that she is unable to make decisions. It means that a wife operates in a manner that aligns with and supports her husband's efforts. A husband should not make decisions alone or operate in a vacuum. In any healthy marriage, the husband and wife will communicate every day about the details of life, both big and small. There should be plenty of give and take from both parties. The husband, whose job it is to serve his wife, should lead in a manner that takes into account the desires, dreams, wishes, and wants of his wife. And the wife, whose job it is to follow her husband, should willingly support her husband's leadership.

The best example for wives is found in Ephesians 5:24, where we read, "As the church submits to Christ, so also wives should submit in everything to their husbands." Just as the church submits to Jesus, so wives are to submit to husbands. That's the model. How does the church operate in relationship with Christ? The church willingly follows Jesus. It comes under his leadership. The church looks to Christ and aligns its ways with his ways. This is not a duty but a delight, due to the steadfast, abundant love of Christ.

It is good to remember that submission is not isolated to wives.

123

In every facet of life, God has ordained an authority structure: children submit to parents, citizens submit to governing authorities, employees submit to their bosses. This same reality exists in the home between a husband and a wife. Finally, Jesus willingly submitted to God the Father, as we hear in his words, "Not my will, but yours be done" (Luke 22:42). Train your daughter to look to Christ as the pattern for followership.

To Be the Household Manager

In Scripture, wives are given a domestic role to manage the daily operations of the home. Some will push back against this idea, suggesting that the woman's role in the home was a cultural expression of the first century, not a biblical expectation for all people of all times. I disagree. The roles of a husband and a wife were mandated by God at creation (Gen. 2:18), and we see this particular aspect of the wife's role mentioned throughout Scripture.

In Proverbs 31:10–31, the wife's focal point is her home. This is summarized by the words of Proverbs 31:27: "She looks well to the ways of her household and does not eat the bread of idleness." Everything that she does, all her business dealings, her early mornings and her late nights, happen with the home in mind. The author of Proverbs 31 tells us that the excellent wife directs her energy and efforts to the household. No idleness on the home front for the Proverbs 31 woman!

In the New Testament, Paul encourages young widows, in 1 Timothy 5:14, to remarry following the death of their husbands, to have children, and to "manage their households." A central component of their role is to direct the affairs of their homes.

In Titus 2:4–5, older women are told to train younger women in six areas: "to love their husbands and children, to be self-controlled, pure, working at home, kind and submissive to their own husbands." Three of these qualities are character related and are important for a daughter when she begins to date. Daughters are to be taught self-control, purity, and kindness. The other three items, of all the skills that Paul could have mentioned, revolve around the home and around a husband and children. Paul teaches that young women need to be trained to work at home. In Titus 2:5, the word *work* means to "busy oneself." It can also mean to take care of something. Young women are to be trained to take care of, and busy themselves with, their future homes.

Why teach your daughter that a wife's role as helpmate centers on managing the home? Because this is an emphasis of Scripture. And, more importantly, God tells you to do it. God instructs older women to teach younger women household management. Daughters need to be given the biblical vision to look after the needs of their homes. Marriage preparation can occur for our daughters at any age, as we give them age-appropriate opportunities to help run the home.

Let me use a twenty-first–century example to illustrate the Bible's teaching. A woman is to marriage what a chief of operations (COO) is to an organization. This is a very important role. Just for fun, I looked up the average salary of a COO; the most common amount I found was in the $170,000 range. The central task of a COO and a wife are one and the same: to handle daily operations. One is corporate, the other domestic. One is fast-paced, requires interaction with emotional adults, and is extremely demanding of one's time and talents. The other is fast-paced, requires interaction with emotional children, and is extremely demanding of one's time and talents. Wives are instructed by God to be the COOs of their homes. They are given a very important job, for it is the home that is the foundation of society and the primary place for the discipleship of children. Your daughter needs a vision to invest in her home and to build into her family. Give your daughter this vision and watch her eyes light up.

It is important for daughters to understand that God has given wives the responsibility to manage the home. One way to help them understand this is to utilize toys as tools to train girls for their role in marriage. I encourage you to be intentional with the toys that you give your daughter. With some forethought, you can use everyday toys to train your daughter for her role as a helpmate who manages her home. For example, give your daughter a toy kitchen and encourage her to learn to be a master chef. We placed old baking utensils, bowls, and cupcake holders in our sandbox, and my daughter can regularly be found baking some wonderful creations for the family to enjoy. As your daughter grows older, she can graduate to cooking regular family meals and having her own baking equipment. If she isn't into baking, give her tools, gardening items, and dolls, as they accomplish a similar outcome.

One of the best ways to teach your daughter to manage her home is to include her in the daily tasks of running a home, such as cooking, cleaning, and managing finances. Combine these experiences with some instruction about her future role of building her home, and your daughter is well on her way to being a helpmate for her family.

To Raise Her Children to Love Jesus

The role of a wife also includes motherhood. Titus 2:4 tells wives to love their children. In 2 Timothy 1:5, Paul describes how Eunice passed on her faith to her son Timothy. Deuteronomy 6:5–7 commands parents to teach their children God's Word.

In Proverbs 1:8–9, wives are given a special role: "Hear, my son, your father's instruction, and forsake not your mother's teaching, for they are garland for your head and pendants for your neck." I refer to Proverbs 1:8 as the Old Testament's job description for the family. In this passage, we read that children are to listen and obey. Fathers are to instruct. Mothers are to teach. Every member of the family is given a clear role.

The Hebrew word *teach* means to point or guide. Mothers are given a biblical role of pointing and guiding their children to Jesus Christ. Their role consists of more than living as a good example in front of their children. They are to verbally teach children to be wise, to apply God's truth to life, to live rightly, and to walk obediently before God. They are also to warn children of the consequences of rebelling against God. (The last two sentences, by the way, are a quick summary of what the book of Proverbs is about.)

According to Proverbs 1:9, a father's instruction and a mother's teaching are desirable like a garland and attractive like a necklace. The analogy of the necklace still has meaning for us, because necklaces are still worn for decoration.[2] Garlands are a different story. When Scripture was written, garlands were awarded to champions for athletic victories; they were also worn to enhance appearance. Today we give athletes gold medals instead of garlands. Thus, the mother who teaches children to treasure Christ is providing them something as valuable as a gold medal—today's equivalent to a garland. God values the role of a wife and mother so highly that her teaching is like an Olympic gold medal for her child to treasure.

A wife's job of investing in her children is legacy worthy. The forging of character in children happens in living rooms, not boardrooms. The passing on of faith from parent to child cannot be delegated to day care, church, or school. A child's heart is shaped, habits are formed, and personality is molded by dozens of small interactions that happen throughout the day. A mother's presence gives her the privilege of being a primary influence on what a child believes and who a child becomes. That is valuable and desirable. Charles Spurgeon does an excellent job describing the importance of this role:

> Those who think that a woman detained at home by her little family is doing nothing think the reverse of what is true. Scarcely can the godly mother quit her home for a place of worship. However, dream not that she is lost to the work of the church. Far from it, she is doing the best possible service for her Lord.
>
> Mothers, the godly training of your offspring is your first and most pressing duty. Christian women, by teaching children the holy Scriptures, are as much fulfilling their part for the Lord as Moses did in judging Israel, or Solomon in building the temple.[3]

2. A necklace would be a great symbolic gift to give to your daughter when you teach this truth.

3. C. H. Spurgeon, *Spiritual Parenting*, rev. ed. (New Kensington, PA: Whitaker House, 2003), 122.

What a wonderful charge to give to our daughters. Raising children and grandchildren who know and love Jesus Christ is an incredible accomplishment worth devoting one's life to. I regularly tell my daughter that she is preparing today to be the spiritual teacher of her home. In order to do this well, daughters need to be trained how to invest spiritually in their families. They can be taught to be prayer warriors and to teach God's Word.

How do we train daughters to teach God's Word to their families? We model it for them. When daughters see parents, and specifically mothers, reading God's Word, talking about God's works, leading their families in devotions, and on their knees in prayer, it leaves an imprint. These actions speak loudly of the importance of these spiritual practices in the life of an individual and family. In my own family, in addition to modeling for our daughters, we give them the opportunity to read the Bible aloud to our family, lead discussion times, and pray during family worship. I want my daughters to be comfortable in this role so that, when they have a family of their own, it is second nature to them. It is a dangerous assumption to believe that our daughters will know how to do this without training.

What Being a Helpmate Is Not

Because of the egalitarian nature of our society, you may struggle with accepting the traditional role of a wife as a helper. When I get pushback on this subject, it typically comes from women who have had a negative experience in a relationship. They were treated as inferior or lived in an oppressive atmosphere. The relationship wasn't a partnership but a hierarchy. It doesn't help when husbands operate with a dictatorial approach to leadership or with the mind-set that they make the money so they make the rules. If this has been your experience, I can understand why you may have strong feelings against the idea of wives as helpmates. But this is not what the Bible teaches, nor is it what I am advocating.

I have no desire for my daughters to marry men who lead with a heavy hand and treat them as second-class citizens. I want my daughters to make a difference for the cause of Christ. I want them to pursue their passions and use their gifts to glorify God and further his kingdom. That happens best through living according to God's good design for the home and embracing the important role that God has given wives. With that in mind, I want to look at three things that being a helpmate is not.

A Helpmate Is Not Solely Wrapped Up in Her Husband and Her Home

Being a helpmate means that a wife's husband and home are her first priority. When we understand what a wife's role is in Scripture, we see that it is not limiting but liberating. It frees women to say yes to the most important priorities and to be intentional with their time and energy. While supporting a husband and a home should be a wife's first priority, this does not have to happen to the exclusion of her involvement in other spheres such as church, community, or work. The one regulates her involvement in the others and helps a husband and wife to discern how much emphasis she should give to areas outside the home at certain stages of life.

A Helpmate Is Not Inferior

Wives have the same immeasurable worth as husbands. Women are created in God's image and are given the rating of "very good" by God (Gen. 1:31). Husbands are to treat wives as the very good creations that they are. As such, there is no place to belittle, abuse, shame, underappreciate, or underutilize the gifting of a wife in marriage. Maybe you've experienced men exercising some form of supremacy over women. If so, this is a distortion of what God created and is to be rejected. While the roles of a husband and wife in marriage differ, their value does not.

To teach this truth to your child, find a padlock and a key. Hold both the lock and the key so that your child can see them, and ask which of the two is more important. Is the key more important than the lock, or the lock more important than the key? Allow some time for discussion. When I do this, children inevitably begin to talk about why the key is important and why the lock is important. Of course, both are very important. Neither could accomplish its purpose without the other. A lock and a key have the same value but different roles, just as a husband and a wife do. A lock is meant to protect something, but it cannot succeed without the help of the key.

All analogies eventually break down, but on a simple level this illustration helps young people to concretely understand the idea of "same value, different role." It helps children to understand that woman is man's complement, not his carbon copy. A woman is to a man what a key is to a lock.

A Helpmate Does Not Have an Interchangeable Role

Many voices in culture are trying to convince girls that the roles of husband and wife are determined by personality or preference rather than by gender-specific personhood. Roles within marriage are treated as an *à la carte* option and left up to personal choice. Couples are encouraged to mix and match as they wish. The cultural value that drives this mind-set is individualism, in which personal preference trumps all.

As a parent, you must recognize and defend your child's heart against an underlying message of our culture: *sameness*. Society is working hard to eliminate any difference between male and female roles. An individualistic, egalitarian culture tells young children to be true to themselves. Self-discovery or self-understanding becomes most important. Girls are warned not to settle for marriage or motherhood or to let these lesser ambitions hold them back from dreaming big and achieving great things.

The message of sameness in marriage roles is a departure from biblical teaching. It is not harmless. It is subtle, and it is pervasive. Without careful recognition and intentional training, it can easily seep into your daughter's belief system and affect how she lives.

What Does This Mean for Working Mothers?

This chapter may have raised some questions. In particular, you may be wondering what a wife's role in the home means for working mothers. Is it outside God's design for mothers to work outside the home?

Let's look to Scripture for this answer. Earlier we looked at the excellent wife from Proverbs 31. She makes it her priority to look after the needs of her home—and she is a savvy businesswoman. "She considers a field and buys it. . . . She perceives that her merchandise is profitable" (Prov. 31:16, 18). The excellent woman contributes to her home through her outside business dealings.

The excellent woman is an example in Scripture of a praiseworthy wife who worked outside the home. That said, her outside work was secondary and supplementary. It supported her efforts at home rather than replacing them.

The workingwoman of Proverbs 31 provides an example of how work and family can be balanced. If an outside job negates a woman's ability to do what God has called her to do in the home, then she should reduce her outside efforts to the degree that is necessary for her to accomplish the running of her home. Different women have different capacities. Some are able to work many hours outside the home and successfully manage both the work and the family worlds. Others struggle to juggle both work and home and should focus greater time and energy on the home front.[4]

Proverbs 14:1 says, "The wisest of women builds her house, but folly with her own hands tears it down." The woman's role is to build her home—not her bank account, career, or name. This is the vision that your daughter needs. She needs a great and grand picture of what it means to be a wife, and that revolves around building a home.

While I have no problem with wives working outside the home, their motives and reasons for doing so are what matter. God has given women a domestic responsibility, and parents need to train their daughters to focus their first and best efforts on this front.

---

4. Preschools, cleaning services, and fast-food restaurants are often used by today's working moms to accomplish what they are not able to manage at home. In addition, husbands are stepping in to help to manage the home. These things, while not bad in themselves, become problematic when they are used to avoid doing what God has called a wife to do.

I want to encourage you to fully equip your daughter for the tasks that God has given her. Prepare your daughter to be a helpmate who is a willing follower, able to manage her home and raise children to love Jesus, and she will be on the path to being a great wife.

The Bible teaches that wives were created by God to be helpers to their husbands. Let us teach this truth to our daughters with clarity and conviction. Let us call our daughters to the high and holy task that God has ordained for them. Let us champion the value of wives and the very important role they are given for God's glory and the advancement of his kingdom.

Courageous Conversations

1. What one word does Genesis 2:18 use to summarize the role of a wife? What does it mean to be a helpmate in marriage?
2. What one command does God repeatedly give to wives in Scripture? What does it mean to submit to a husband?
   a. 1 Peter 3:1–2
   b. Colossians 3:18
   c. Ephesians 5:22
3. Study Ephesians 5:22–33. What do the words "as unto the Lord," from Ephesians 5:22, suggest about a wife's role?
4. What example should a wife keep in mind as she operates as a willing follower to her husband? How extensive is her followership to be? See Ephesians 5:24. What limits are placed on a wife's submission in Acts 5:29?
5. Read the following passages. What do they teach a woman about her role as a wife?
   a. Proverbs 31:26, 28
   b. 1 Peter 3:1–6
6. Study Titus 2:4–5. What three items that focus on the home are mothers to teach daughters? How do these three responsibilities apply to a woman's role as a wife?
7. Read Proverbs 14:1 and 31:27. What do these passages teach about the role of a wife?

8. What is a key component of a wife's role found in the following verses?
    a. Proverbs 31:10; 31
    b. Proverbs 1:8–9
    c. 2 Timothy 1:5
    d. Deuteronomy 6:5–7
9. Ask your child to summarize the role of a wife in one sentence.

10

Preparing Your Child for Singleness

Finding Satisfaction in God Rather Than Marriage

As we talk about marriage with our children, it is natural to be concerned about whom they will marry. But to be concerned about only their spouse in marriage is shortsighted. We should be just as concerned with preparing our children to *be marriageable*. This means you will need to do some heart work with your child.

Here are two keys that will help you instruct your child on how to date in a God-honoring way.

Put God First

What difference does it make when two people come together seeking their satisfaction from Christ rather than in each other? The pre-dating years are critical years for you to help your child treasure Jesus Christ more than anything else in life. During this time, your goal is to fuel your child's passion for Christ.

Putting God first puts everything else into proper perspective and enables a young person to love a future spouse in a way that is good and godly. It also prevents a future spouse from becoming a God-replacement and from operating as the ultimate provider of your child's needs. That honor is for God alone.

Your aim during the single years is to *help your child to get his or her affections in the proper order*. The first and greatest commandment in Scripture is to love the Lord God with all your heart (see Luke 10:27). Then we are to love others. We must guard against misplaced affections that reverse God's order.

Marriage is not your child's key to happiness. Jesus is. You ought to elevate and celebrate marriage with your children, but not to the point at which marriage becomes the source of a young person's happiness in life. Pursuing from others what only God can provide for us leads to frustration, because other people can't deliver. Therefore, encourage your child to find his or her ultimate satisfaction in Jesus.

Marriage can easily become a Jesus-substitute for a young person. If marriage becomes your child's primary source of satisfaction or means of joy, then it has become an idol for your child and is replacing God in his or her life. And it will always disappoint. This is precisely what Richard and Sharon Phillips, authors of *Holding Hands, Holding Hearts: Recovering a Biblical View of Christian Dating*, point out.

> If God is my portion, if God is the true source of my joy, and if it is God who will fulfill me, then I am free to be a companion instead of a consumer. That is, because of what I receive from God I can give to another person instead of always taking. . . . Having their needs met by God, they enjoy a relationship of service to one another. This is the dynamic that distinguishes a healthy, godly relationship from a worldly, idolatrous one.[1]

---

1. Richard D. Phillips & Sharon L. Phillips, *Holding Hands, Holding Hearts: Recovering a Biblical View of Christian Dating* (Phillipsburg, NJ: P&R Publishing, 2006), 58, 63.

American culture tells our children that marriage is a means of self-satisfaction—a way to make themselves happy and have their needs met. The problem with this thinking is that it is idolatry. True joy and ultimate satisfaction can come only from Jesus. When our souls seek satisfaction from any other source, even marriage, that source operates as a Jesus-replacement.

We cannot love a spouse well if we don't love Jesus first. The state of our love for God directly affects how we love others. "Only when we [find] our ultimate satisfaction in God are we able to relate rightly to one another."[2] This is why the Bible tells us that if we seek first the kingdom of God, all these things will be added (see Matt. 6:33). Your child's greatest aim is to love the *Lord*, not a boyfriend or girlfriend, with all of his or her heart.

Be Content in Singleness

Have you considered that your child may never get married? If this is the case, will he or she feel incomplete or unhappy? What if your child is called by God to be a modern-day Jeremiah? God asked Jeremiah to remain single as a visible sign to a lost people of their need to repent and turn to the Lord (see Jer. 16:1–4). In Matthew 19:12, Jesus used the picture of a eunuch to illustrate a person who foregoes marriage for the sake of the kingdom of God. These two examples suggest that it is normal for some people to willingly give up the blessing of marriage in order to serve God. Barry Danylak, author of *Redeeming Singleness*, states, "Singleness, like salvation itself, is an open call to live a distinctive life for the sake of the kingdom of God, and those who have a sense of their innate ability to respond to the call *should* do so."[3]

What if God wants to further his kingdom through your child's singleness? Will you and your child be prepared to embrace his or her

2. Ibid., 56.

3. Barry Danylak, *Redeeming Singleness: How the Storyline of Scripture Affirms the Single Life* (Wheaton, IL: Crossway, 2010), 199.

single life with contentment and joy? Will your child intentionally invest the extra time available from his or her singleness for God's glory, or will he or she waste it in frivolous self-pursuits?

All children begin their lives unmarried and will be single for a portion of time. In addition, even if they marry, they may become single again due to the death of a spouse. We want our children to be able to say, with the psalmist, "You are my Lord; I have no good apart from you" (Ps. 16:2). *Your job is to train your child to find his or her satisfaction in Jesus instead of in marriage.*

Let's take a few moments to consider what the Bible teaches about singleness.

Singleness Is Not Abnormal

Singleness is not an abnormality to be fixed or a sickness to be cured. There is nothing wrong with being single. As we teach our children about marriage, we want to guard against making marriage into the eleventh commandment. Paul's words in 1 Corinthians 7:32–35 suggest that marriage and singleness are an issue of freedom in Christ. The New Testament affirms singleness as a gift and a valued lifestyle for a believer (see 1 Cor. 7:7). Some young people may be gifted with singleness and divinely enabled to serve God in their singleness for a specific purpose.

Marriage Is Not for Eternity

It is helpful to remember that there is no earthly marriage in eternity. Jesus taught that the ultimate state for every believer in the age to come does not include marriage (see Luke 20:34–36). Earthly marriage is temporary. It will be replaced with our marriage to the Lamb and celebrated at the wedding feast of heaven (Rev. 19:6–9; Matt. 22:2–14). The purpose of earthly marriage will have been fulfilled. There will be no bearing of children and no need to be fruitful and multiply in eternity. Marriage will no longer need to point to Christ's work on the cross. The picture will be replaced with the real thing. Every person in heaven will experience, in a greater degree, the close companionship that marriage provides. There will no longer be sin to disrupt and destroy relationships, and thus the depth of our fellowship will be like nothing we have ever experienced before. The Bible speaks of heaven as being better than anything that any person can imagine. There, the joys of worshipping the Lord will dwarf the pleasures of earthly marriage.

If you have an intimate marriage, it is hard to imagine existing in any other state. But the Bible teaches that in heaven, rather than being husband and wife, you will be brother and sister in Christ, rejoicing together before Jesus. Will husbands and wives share a special bond and recall life memories together? I would like to think they will, but I cannot definitively answer.

Singleness is the ultimate state for every believer. Because it is your future state, you should seek to understand and appreciate it. If God calls your child to a life of singleness, your child should embrace that life with contentment. As parents, we ought to avoid expressing disappointment if this is the path that God has for our children. Instead, let us support our children in this self-sacrificing endeavor.

Marriage Isn't Necessary for Happiness

Jesus was single. He never experienced a wedding anniversary or the joys or struggles of marriage. He never had children or the companionship of a spouse. Yet Jesus was the happiest person to ever live. He knew the love of the Father and lived in obedience to his will. Jesus did not need marriage in order to be happy. Neither does your child. If ever a young person feels poorly about being single, he or she can look to Christ as an example.

Singleness Brings Benefits

Paul, the greatest of all the apostles, was single and content with his singleness. Multiple times Paul encouraged believers to remain single. Here is one example: "He who marries his betrothed does well, and he who refrains from marriage will do even better" (1 Cor. 7:38). Paul used his singleness to serve God. There was intentionality to his singleness.

The Bible points out that one of the primary benefits of

singleness is a heightened ability to invest in God's work. Single individuals do not have the distraction of family and are able to serve in ways that married individuals cannot. Single individuals are free from the time demands of marriage and parenting. Those who are single are free to invest a greater amount of time into serving the Lord. Singleness can be a great blessing to the church and a great blessing to your child. For this purpose, it should be elevated and celebrated just as marriage is.

As you work through the questions at the end of this chapter, explore with your child the possibility that God may be calling him or her to embrace intentional singleness for the cause of Christ (see 1 Cor. 7:32–35).

Paul provides one critical criterion to help a young person determine whether he or she should remain single. In 1 Corinthians 7:9, he states, "If they cannot exercise self-control, they should marry. For it is better to marry than to burn with passion." It is good for a young person to remain single if, and only if, that person remains sexually pure. Is your child able to have complete control over his or her sexual life? If young people lack sexual self-control, this indicates that they should pursue marriage, since God has designed marriage as the only place for your child to exercise sexual activity.

While it is helpful to consider what the Bible has to say about singleness, it is good to remember that marriage will be the norm for most children. Jesus and Paul did not advocate singleness for everyone. They simply presented singleness as a good and God-honoring option for some individuals to prayerfully consider. God may be calling your child to remain single for the sake of furthering his kingdom. This is possible only if your child's ultimate satisfaction is found in Christ.

Courageous Conversations

1. What do the following verses teach about priorities and the place of dating in someone's life?
   a. Matthew 6:33
   b. Luke 10:27
2. Have you ever considered that God may be calling you to a life of singleness in order to serve him? What are your thoughts about that possibility?
3. Read Jeremiah 16:1–4 and Matthew 19:12. What do we learn about singleness from the example of these individuals?
4. Read Psalm 16:2. What does this passage teach about finding our satisfaction in God rather than marriage?
5. What does the Bible teach about singleness?
   a. 1 Corinthians 7:7
   b. 1 Corinthians 7:32–35
   c. 1 Corinthians 7:38
   d. Luke 20:34–36
6. According to 1 Corinthians 7:9, a young person should pursue marriage for what reason?

PART 3

SEX AND PURITY

11

WHAT BIBLICAL TRUTHS DOES YOUR CHILD NEED TO KNOW ABOUT SEX?

Remembering God's Good Plan and Purpose

"Mom, what is sex?" The question caught Emily off guard. After all, her daughter was only nine years old. This wasn't a topic that Emily was prepared to talk about, so she told her daughter they would talk later. Meanwhile, Emily asked me, "Can you recommend a book or website that would be appropriate for me to use to talk with my daughter about sex?"

As with Emily, our first instinct is to look for a book from an expert. There are helpful books out there.[1] Hopefully, this is one of those books! However, God in his wisdom has given us a comprehensive, practical resource to use with our children for this purpose. That resource is the Bible. It is intended by God to be the primary source of guidance about sex for both those who are single and those who are married.

---

1. See, for instance, Carolyn Nystrom, *Before I Was Born*, rev. ed. (Pontiac, IL: NavPress, 2007).

Did you know that the Bible devotes an entire book to the celebration of sex within marriage? This book is inspired by the Holy Spirit, without error, and authoritative. If you haven't guessed, the book I'm referencing is the Song of Songs. Unfortunately, it is rarely included in children's Bibles or teenage Bible studies. Few parents have read portions of the Song of Songs to their children, meaning that most young people hear only the "don'ts" from Scripture without receiving a picture of what married sex should look like.

C. J. Mahaney writes,

> Solomon's Song of Songs is an entire book of the Bible devoted to the promotion of sexual intimacy within the covenant of marriage. It's an eight-chapter feast of unbridled, uninhibited, joyous immersion in verbal and physical expressions of passion between a man and a woman.
>
> Not a couple of verses. Not a chapter or two. God didn't consider that enough. He decided to give us a whole book!
>
> But can the Song of Songs really be about sex? Isn't the Bible about, well, spiritual stuff?
>
> It sure is. And sexual intimacy within marriage has profound spiritual significance.[2]

Here's a taste of what the Song of Songs says about physical affection and marriage:

- *Physical affection*: "Let him kiss me with the kisses of his mouth" (1:2).
- *More physical affection*: "His left hand is under my head, and his right hand embraces me" (2:6).
- *And more physical affection*: "My beloved has gone down to his garden . . . to graze in the gardens and to gather lilies" (6:2).

2. C. J. Mahaney, *Sex, Romance, and the Glory of God: What Every Christian Husband Needs to Know* (Wheaton, IL: Crossway, 2004), 10.

- *Conflict resolution*: "Catch the foxes for us, the little foxes that spoil the vineyards" (2:15).
- *Sexual longing*: "On my bed by night I sought him whom my soul loves" (3:1).
- *Sexual talk*: "Behold, you are beautiful, my love" (4:1).
- *Sexual anticipation*: "My beloved put his hand to the latch, and my heart was thrilled within me" (5:4).
- *Sexual delight*: "How beautiful and pleasant you are, O loved one, with all your delights!" (7:6).

It's unlikely that your child is taught a biblical view of sex anywhere else. Society is happy to celebrate immoral sex. We parade it on TV, place it before young eyes in ads, and sing about it in songs. Meanwhile, married sex—the kind of sex that God fashioned, the kind that will blow away any one-night stand—is kept hidden out of sight. As a result, young people are left to wonder if married sex is bland and boring. Sadly, few children have a biblical vision for sex within the context of marriage.

Most parents recognize that children need help in order to think biblically about sex. We know that we need to talk with our children about it. As in every area of life, we want our children to submit their sexual practices to God. We know that sex has the potential to either be a great blessing or cause great heartache for our children. We want our children to have a proper understanding of God's purpose for sex. Our struggle lies not with our willingness but with knowing what to talk about with our children.

This chapter will provide a biblical foundation that you can use to discuss sex with your child. It will provide you with key truths for your first in-depth "talk" on the subject of sex. Your job is to give your child a God-honoring, biblical, rock-their-world vision for sex.

In the next chapter, I'll show you a passage in the Bible that you can use when you sit down to have a second "talk" with your child. It will give you some more details for child-appropriate teaching on this subject. Remember, you should have more than one talk with your child about sex! To start, though, here are four truths about sex that your child needs to hear.

God Is the Authority

The first thing we learn about sex from the Bible is that *God created it* (see Gen. 2:24). Don't skip over this point with your children.

Why is this important? God is the world's sexual authority. If God created sex, then he gets to tell us how to understand and enjoy it. God decides what is sexually appropriate and what is not. He gets to call the shots. He is the one in charge. He knows what is best for us, what we need sexually, and when we need it.

The challenge is in figuring out how to help a child conform his or her sexual practices to God's ways. The answer to this challenge has less to do with abstinence pledges and more to do with trusting God's authority. The sexual battle your child will eventually face will not be won or lost because you put the right kinds of dating boundaries in place or because your child wears a purity ring—although these things can help. Your child's future sexual practices will be heavily determined by one thing: *whom your child decides is the sexual authority of his or her life.*

Kenny Luck, a pastor at Saddleback Church, wrote a helpful article on what he calls "sexual atheism." In it, he describes the sexual practices of a growing number of Christian young people who compartmentalize their faith from their sexuality and decide to be their own sexual authorities. "Sexual atheism" is the mind-set that God can speak into some areas of life but not sexuality. "It is the ultimate oxymoron," Luck writes. Sexual atheists believe in God while at the same time believing that he "should not, cannot or will not inform their thinking or living sexually."[3]

Your job as a mom, dad, or grandparent is to convince your

---

3. Kenny Luck, "Sexual Atheism: Christian Dating Data Reveals a Deeper Spiritual Malaise," *Charisma News*, April 9, 2014, www.charismanews.com/opinion /43436-sexual-atheism-christian-dating-data-reveals-a-deeper-spiritual-malaise.

child that God does have a lot to say about sex, that what he says is of great consequence, and that it should inform their sexual practices. When it comes to sex, there is no better source and no higher authority than Scripture. God did not leave something as powerful as sex for us to figure out. He is not ambiguous about what he expects sexually from single and married people.

Who will be your child's sexual authority? Will it be God—or will it be himself or herself? When it comes to sexual purity, the main battleground isn't the bedroom or the computer screen. Those are just the playgrounds. The real battleground is the heart. This is where our children will decide either to bend the knee or to go their own way. This is where our children will ask, "Did God really say . . . ?" as it relates to their sexual practices. This is where our children will weigh their own desires against God's decrees. We want to help our children understand that God's ways are always the best ways. His words are true, trustworthy, and timeless. His plan is safe and sure. As the creator of sex, he knows best.

Sex Has a Purpose

The second thing we learn is that *sex has a purpose*. By God's design, sex has very specific functions in marriage.

What is the purpose of sex? Ask your child that question. We don't want our children to define sex in terms of self-fulfillment, which is what culture says is the purpose of sex. Just about everything that children see or hear sends the message that sex exists to make them happy and bring them pleasure. Sex does those things, but it also does much more than that.

God created sex to accomplish four purposes.

For Children

If you ask your child what the purpose of sex is, he or she will probably tell you that it is for making babies. That is correct! The first command that God gave Adam and Eve was to be fruitful and multiply (see Gen. 1:28). How would they do that? Sex. In a roundabout way, the first command in the Bible is a command to have sex. Sex is the God-designed means of making a baby in the context of marriage.

If God created sex for making babies, then it is good that our children embrace this purpose for their marriage, should God choose to bless them this way. Pay attention to how you talk about this topic with your child. It's easy to send a mixed message—one that undercuts this God-designed purpose for sex. What would that sound like? "Be fruitful and multiply, but not too much." "Children are a gift from God—but are best postponed until after a career has been established or debt has been paid off." Champion children and show your child that the Bible connects sex and childbearing.

To Strengthen a Marriage

In Genesis 2:24, God states that a man and a woman are to be "one flesh." This suggests that sex is central to marriage. It suggests that God expects a husband and a wife to have sex. This is his plan and his desire. Of course, having sex isn't the only way that a couple operates as one. But it is the primary way. And it is what God had in mind when he used the word "flesh." God could have left this word out. But notice how it would change things if he did. He could have said that "a man will leave his father and mother and hold fast to his wife, and they shall become one" (Gen. 2:24). God doesn't just tell couples to be one. He tells them to be one flesh. That places a strong emphasis on the physical elements of a marriage relationship.

Not only does God emphasize sex in marriage, he commands it. In Genesis 2:24 God says, "Become one flesh." Teach this expectation to your children. Talk through why couples should work hard to build and maintain this area of their marriage. Tell your child how sex has strengthened your marriage. If you need some talking points, you might consider telling your child that it connects a husband and wife on a deep level. It unites them. Sex is God's glue to bring together, to bind together, and to hold together. It strengthens couples spiritually. It melts away conflict. It helps to minimize disagreements and differences. In short, it helps a couple to be one in all areas of life.

To Protect a Marriage

Next tell your child that *sex within marriage should be free and frequent.* Sex in your child's future marriage should be just as common as eating and bathing.

In 1 Corinthians 7:5, we see Paul's expectation that sex within marriage should happen with regular consistency. He says that couples should decide together when not to have sex and that these times should be few in number and short in length. He gives the example of a husband and wife deciding to not have sex so that they can devote themselves to prayer. Other reasons may include an extended illness, travel, or other major life events.

Why should married couples have sex often? Frequent sex is a defense against sexual temptation (see 1 Cor. 7:5) and against other enemies that seek to destroy a marriage. It protects both individuals from sexual sin. God uses frequent sex to help couples remain faithful to each other and sexually pure in thought and action. Eliminate or limit sex in marriage and the potential for unfaithfulness rises considerably. Couples who have infrequent sex open themselves up to countless temptations.

There are to be no strings attached to sex in marriage. Sex is not to be used as a weapon to get what one wants. It is not to be withheld when a spouse is angry or tired. Sex should be pursued in marriage when the relationship is strong and when it is struggling, when the couple feels warm fuzzies and when they don't, when they are well rested and when they are exhausted, when they are newly married and when they have been married for decades, when it is convenient and when it is inconvenient, when they are getting along and when they are disagreeing. In short, sex is to be free and frequent in a marriage.

To Enjoy

Sex is God's gift to a husband and a wife. It's fun. Married sex, the kind God intended, is wonderful. Your child should know this.

You don't need to dive into specifics about this area of your marriage unless you want to. You do need to help your child understand that what the world offers outside marriage is a shadow of what God intends within marriage. If our children seek pleasure without seeking to please the Lord in the process, they won't experience what it means to be naked and not ashamed (see Gen. 2:25). Our children won't know the pleasure of rejoicing in the wife of their youth (see Prov. 5:18). Part of saying no to sexual sin is learning to have the self-control to wait for something better. According to the Bible, married sex is better than unmarried sex (see Prov. 5). In fact, it's not even close. Tell your children this!

God created sex to be enjoyed. God could have given us the same feeling in our genitals that we have in our fingers. But he didn't do that. He gave us thousands of extra nerve endings in our genitals for the sole purpose of generating pleasure. God designed the human body for pleasure in sex. Children need to learn to receive this gift, pursue it within marriage, and enjoy the wife or husband of their youth.

Sex within Marriage Is Good

What was your view of sex when you were a young person? Did you wrinkle your nose at it? When you got married, did you feel like you were doing something wrong when you had sex? Were you consumed by it? Was it all you could think about? Or did you appreciate it for the purpose that God created it for?

Helping our children to have a correct view of sex is no easy task. Plenty of children have a distorted view of sex, and this makes a big difference—especially when they get married. Young people tend to hold one of three different views of sex.[4] Knowing these categories will be helpful for you as you think about which of them your child most likely embraces.

4. Adapted from Matt Capps, "What Does the Bible Teach About Sex?," The Gospel Project, November 8, 2013, https://www.gospelproject.com/2013/11/08/bible-teach-sex/.

Sex Is Gross

Plenty of young people view sex negatively. The way that parents or pastors talk about the subject has left them thinking that sex is bad. They are frequently reminded that sex outside marriage is wrong, that STDs are lurking to get them, and that unmarried pregnancy is God's consequence for sin. They are told that sex will destroy their lives. As rules and consequences are emphasized, young people develop a confused and poor view of sex, perceiving it as dirty and disgusting. A child who is raised this way may avoid sexual exploits while single but also struggle within marriage to embrace the gift of sex that God has given a husband and wife. Parents need a biblically balanced approach that addresses the negative consequences of sexual sin but also the positive joys of married sex, which I address in the next chapter. Avoid using fear or guilt to encourage your child to pursue sexual purity.

Sex Is God

At the other end of the spectrum is when sex is celebrated too much. People with this view do not recognize the boundaries that God has created for sex. They seek the joys of sex outside its God-designed context. Sex assumes an unhealthy place in their mind or life. Some people become obsessed with it. They can't stop thinking about it; they can't stop pursuing it—either in real life or through pornography. They have bought into the lie that sex exists solely for pleasure, and the outcome is the pursuit of personal fulfillment through sex. Sex is made into their object of worship—an idol.

Sex Is Good

Paul writes, "Everything created by God is good, and nothing is to be rejected if it is received with thanksgiving" (1 Tim. 4:4). That may seem like an odd passage to reference in relation to sex, but it's not. Sex comes from God. It was created by him. According to Paul, it is to be received with thanksgiving. Within the safety of marriage, sex is good. It strengthens a relationship and deepens trust. The Old Testament joyfully affirms the beauty of sex in marriage. The New

Testament encourages married couples to view sex as a self-sacrificial commitment that is part of God's calling to live our lives for his glory. Sex within the context of marriage is sex in the service of God. It is meant to produce children, strengthen a marriage, protect a marriage from unfaithfulness, and give enjoyment. And this is good.

We want our children to have a balanced and biblical view of sex. That means that we need to help them understand that sex within marriage is good.

Sex Is Never an End in Itself

Sex is more than a pleasurable activity. It has a deeper meaning than the relationship between a man and a woman. Sex reminds us of Jesus' love. The deep love that a couple express to each other through physical intimacy is meant to be a reminder of the even deeper love that Jesus has for the world, expressed through his death on the cross. John Piper makes a similar point: "God made us powerfully sexual so that he would be more deeply knowable. We were given the power to know each other sexually so that we might have some hint of what it will be like to know Christ supremely."[5] Properly understood, sex proclaims the gospel from one spouse to another. It points a couple heavenward. It keeps their eyes focused on Christ and his sacrifice.

Courageous Conversations

1. Read Genesis 2:24. What does "one flesh" mean? What does this tell us about who created sex? At what point are a husband and wife to become one flesh—before or after they are married? Why is the order important?
2. Read 2 Timothy 3:16–17 and John 8:31–32. What do these passages teach about God's authority over all things, including sex?

5. John Piper and Justin Taylor, eds., *Sex and the Supremacy of Christ* (Wheaton, IL: Crossway Books, 2005), 30.

3. Did you know that the Bible has an entire book devoted to the celebration of sex in marriage? Let's get a taste of what the Song of Songs says about physical affection and marriage. Read the following verses:

    a. Song of Songs 1:2

    b. Song of Songs 2:6

    c. Song of Songs 2:15

    d. Song of Songs 3:1

    e. Song of Songs 4:1

    f. Song of Songs 5:4

    g. Song of Songs 6:2

    h. Song of Songs 7:6

4. What did you learn about sex from the Song of Songs?

5. God created sex in marriage for a purpose. What four purposes do we see for sex throughout the following verses?

    a. Genesis 1:27–28.

    b. Genesis 2:24. How does physical affection strengthen a marriage and lead to oneness?

    c. 1 Corinthians 7:5. Based on this passage, what are two reasons why couples might not come together as one flesh? How long should that last? Why is it good to come together again?

    d. Proverbs 5:18 and Song of Songs 7:6.

6. According to 1 Timothy 4:4, how should you view sex inside marriage?

7. God wants you to submit your sexual practices to him. Is that something you are willing to do? Why or why not?

How to Have "the Talk"

Using Proverbs 5

Matt's hand shot up in the middle of a marriage seminar, and he blurted out, "How do I talk to my child about sex?" After probing further, I learned that Matt's oldest child was in middle school and he was feeling pressure to have "the talk." Matt, like so many other parents, was reluctant to talk to his child about sex. "I really don't know what to say, and I don't want to plant thoughts in my child's mind."

In the last chapter, we talked about how to communicate God's good plan and purpose for sex to your child. Now that you are ready to show him or her that God is the authority on sex, that sex has a purpose, that sex within marriage is good, and that sex is never an end in itself, you are prepared to talk in detail about sex with your child. Did you know that God, in his wisdom, provided you with an example to follow? Proverbs 5:1–23 records a father having the talk with his son. Over the years, I've trained many parents to talk with their children about sex using this chapter.

Preparing to Teach Your Child

Read Proverbs 5

The first thing you need to do is to read Proverbs 5:1–23 and become familiar with the passage. Try doing that right now and then returning to this book.

One of the first responses I get from parents about this chapter is that Proverbs 5 is inappropriate for young people. If you are hesitant to read and discuss this passage with your child, consider three things.

- *Proverbs 5 is written to a child (see vv. 1, 7).* This should eliminate any fear that this passage or subject matter is inappropriate for children. It should also lead to confidence that you are instructing your child with the right content in the right way. You should be comfortable addressing topics with your children that God addresses with children in the Bible.
- *Proverbs 5 is inspired by God.* He chose to talk to children about this topic. I trust that God knows better than anyone else what a child needs to hear.
- *Proverbs assumes that a difficult sexual struggle will occur in your child's life.* If this is the case, you must teach your child what the Bible says about sexuality and check in with him or her instead of waiting for your child to approach you. Every child needs guidance and accountability from a parent in this area of life. Proverbs 5 shows you how to do this.

Your child can handle Proverbs 5. He or she may giggle or blush, but you won't be planting ideas that will make your child sex-crazy. How do I know? I've taught Proverbs 5 to hundreds of children aged K–12, including to my own children.

What's the alternative? Come up with your own talking points? Seek a source outside the Bible? Remain silent on the subject? Remember, the Bible claims to be sufficient for all matters of life, which includes giving your child a Christ-centered view of sex. Why not use the Bible for the purpose for which God gave it to you?

Ask What Your Child Knows about Sex

Next, ask your child what he or she knows about sex. What has he seen? What has she done? What has been done to him? Your child probably knows more about sex and has seen and thought more about sex than you realize. He or she may even have experienced more than you realize. It's helpful to know this before diving into Proverbs 5, as it may influence what you say or how you talk about the subject.

The longer I've been in ministry with young people, the more I hear about sexual experiences that young children are frequently exposed to. If your child has had a sexual experience, get it on the table. No doubt your child is feeling shame and has lots of questions. Help him or her to understand what has happened through the lens of the Bible. If you don't feel equipped, ask a pastor for help.[1]

Never shut down a discussion by getting angry when your child opens up, asks a question, or shares a doubt. Create a safe environment. Show love and embody grace without excusing sin. If your child has experimented sexually, he or she is probably terrified to tell you. Try to stay away from condemnation and to listen. Save instruction and admonition for a later time.

Before reading Proverbs 5 with your child, give your child permission to ask questions. The older your child gets, the more questions he or she will have about sex. Expect curiosity. Assume that your child has questions. Your child will ask questions if he or she is given permission to and feels safe. Your goal is to be an askable parent and to give honest, age-appropriate answers according to the Bible, such as the content covered in the previous chapter.

1. If your child has disobeyed God sexually, then invite your child to confess his or her sin to God. He promises to forgive those who humbly confess sin. Your child may benefit from reading Psalm 51, which recounts the sexual sin of David with Bathsheba and provides an example of confession for our children to follow. Share the gospel with your child as well. Jesus paid the penalty for sin, and all sexual sinners who believe in him will have new life. When they repent, they will no longer bear a black mark in God's eyes but are given a clean, fresh start.

Discuss Proverbs 5 with Your Child

Finally, read Proverbs 5 with your child and discuss it. The questions at the end of this chapter may be helpful for this purpose. Here are a few things to keep in mind.

- The younger the child, the more conservative you should be with your words and the more general with details.
- Proverbs 5 is somber at the beginning and joyful at the end. As you teach this passage, your child should feel the weight of sin and know that there are costs and consequences of sexual sin. But don't leave your child there. The passage is also joyful, celebrating the benefits of sex in marriage. Remember what was discussed in the previous chapter and try to achieve a balance.
- Proverbs 5 does not focus on male or female anatomy or mention the mechanics of sex. Instead, the author covers temptation, the cost of sexual sin, and the joys of sex in marriage. Let that inform your conversation with your child.[2]

What to Teach a Child about Sex

Sexual Temptation Will Come (Prov. 5:3–4)

Your child is going to face a sexual battle. He or she needs to know how to respond *before* entering the battlefield. Sexual temptation is appealing. From a distance it looks good—much like honey (see Prov. 5:3). That shouldn't fool your child. When tempted, your child will be shown the sweet, not the sour; the pleasure, not the poison. Sin is a lot like cotton candy—empty and unfulfilling. It tastes good for a moment, but it always leaves a person feeling empty. Sin looks appealing but delivers its promises only momentarily—if

2. That doesn't mean you shouldn't cover anatomy or mechanics—just that these are supporting subject matters. If you are looking for a helpful resource that covers these topics and more, I recommend Dennis Rainey's CD series, *Passport-2Purity* (Little Rock: FamilyLife, 2012). This resource provides a clear explanation of sex that will generate fruitful discussion between a parent and child.

it delivers them at all. What helps a young person to say no to sexual temptation?

Sexual Decisions Have Consequences (Prov. 5:5–6)

I like this father's tactics. He encourages his son to look into the future and imagine what will happen when he makes certain decisions. The father uses the adulterous woman as an example and says, "She does not ponder the path of life" (Prov. 5:6). Essentially, the father has found a case study, shown it to his son, and exposed the consequences of sexual sin. That is a smart dad.

Proverbs 5 operates as a warning, showing children what to expect if they choose this path in life. Use this passage to persuade your child to avoid destructive decisions that lead him or her away from Jesus. There are three things your child should know about sexual sin.

- *It is bitter (Prov. 5:4).* It tastes horrible. If you really want to drive this point home, find a bitter drink (such as diluted vinegar or salt water) and have your child take a sip. Tell him or her that this is what sexual sin is like—but magnified exponentially.
- *It leads to death (Prov. 5:5).* Sexual sin is not freeing. It costs people their lives. For some, the result is sexual addiction. For others, it is an STD. Sin always results in death, never life. It steals joy and enslaves.
- *Sexual sin is a path to hell (Prov. 5:5).* If this doesn't get your child's attention, I don't know what will. Explain to your child that his or her eternity is at stake. It is a serious matter to live in rebellion to Jesus Christ.

At the heart of being a disciple of Jesus Christ is learning to obey all God's commands—including his commands for our sexuality.

Sex Has Limits

It is worthwhile to read Proverbs 5 out loud, from beginning to end, and to work with your child to identify God's limitations on sex as you encounter them in the passage. In case your child gets stuck, I've listed a few of them here.

- Sex is to occur only within the context of marriage, never outside marriage (vv. 1–6, 20).
- Sex is meant for a man and a woman. God speaks only in heterosexual language, never homosexual language (vv. 1, 18).
- Sex is never to be shared with anyone but a spouse (v. 17). This eliminates everything from cohabitation to one-night stands and the idea of open marriage.

Recognizing the parameters of sexual activity is important because, increasingly, unmarried young people who claim to love Jesus are not living according to God's sexual standards. For example, there is a growing trend for couples to be sexually intimate if they are in a committed relationship that is headed toward marriage. During premarital counseling, a couple said to me, "We love each other, and that should be enough in God's eyes. Marriage isn't needed if there is love." Proverbs 5 exposes this line of thinking as erroneous and sinful.

God's standard is for a husband to sexually rejoice in the *wife* of his youth, not in his fiancée or serious girlfriend. Proverbs 5 helps a young person to understand that a serious monogamous relationship should not be treated the same as a marriage. Just because a couple plans to get married doesn't mean they should live like they are married before their wedding day. Sexual longings are to be fulfilled in marriage. No exceptions.

Paul echoes this same idea in 1 Corinthians 6:15–20. He tells the Corinthians that having sex outside the covenant of marriage is harmful to the bodies and souls of both parties. Then he provides this instruction: "Flee from sexual immorality" (1 Cor. 6:18). Your child needs to hear that loud and clear. It's what the father in Proverbs 5:8 said to his son: "Keep your way far from her, and do not go near the door of her house."

Sexual Sin Has a Price Tag (Prov. 5:8–14)

At the beginning of the discussion, the father in Proverbs 5 tells his son to expect death and destruction if he pursues sex with a woman he is not married to. Apparently, the son needs another round of warnings, because the father adds four more consequences for pursuing sex with someone who is not your spouse. Here are the price tags:

- *Honor (v. 9).* Sexual sin brings about the loss of respect in the eyes of others due to a stained character. Sexual sin puts a black mark on the sinner's reputation. Lack of integrity always leads to a loss in credibility.
- *Time (vv. 9–10).* In adultery, time that could have gone to building a marriage is used to destroy a marriage. People who sin sexually use time to inflict wounds on themselves and on those they love.
- *Wealth (v. 10).* The unfaithful give their resources to others. Verse 10 says, "Their labors go to the house of another." Sexual sin may have a financial cost. It may cost the sinner a job. Or he or she may need to pay child support. Sexual sin always carries a spiritual price tag, but it may also include a financial cost.
- *Regret (vv. 11–13).* Those who sin sexually must live their whole lives knowing that they made a foolish choice. In the end, their sin may bring them to utter ruin both in this life and in eternity (see v. 14).

The costs of sexual sin ought to be at the forefront of your child's mind when he or she is faced with sexual temptation. Our hope as parents is that our children will be able to obliterate the false promise of sexual pleasure through their understanding of the costs of sexual sin and the knowledge that a greater *yes* awaits them.

Sex Should Be Enjoyed in Marriage (Prov. 5:18–19)

In Proverbs 5:18, God tells young people how to have a blessed, or happy, marriage. I've never met a couple who didn't want this!

Leverage this desire with your child. God has only two things for a young person to remember:

- *Rejoice in your spouse (v. 18).* Plenty of married people criticize and complain about their spouses and wish that they would change. Rather than complain about the negative traits or habits that a spouse may have, a young person is to purposefully rejoice in all the positive things that his or her spouse brings to the marriage. God commands young people to rejoice in their spouses. They are to choose joy. They are to celebrate the good things. Happiness in marriage has more to do with a choice than it does with a feeling.
- *Have lots of sex in marriage (v. 19).* Spouses are to enjoy each other physically, and this helps them to maintain marital faithfulness. To make his point, God uses a strong word picture. God tells couples to be "intoxicated with love" in verse 19. In order to be intoxicated with alcohol, a person must drink a considerable amount over a period of time. As alcohol is to a drunk, so sex ought to be to a marriage. "At all times" and "intoxicated" suggest there is to be a regularity and consistency to physical expressions of love in marriage.

Sexual Urges Are to Be Controlled (Prov. 5:23)

In Proverbs 5, the father challenges his son to discipline his sexual urges. The exact words of the father are, "He dies for lack of discipline" (v. 23). Your child needs to learn to discipline his or her affections. One of the most important things for you to teach your child is self-control (see Titus 2:5–6). The Bible teaches young people to run from, rather than embrace, sexual urges that do not align with God's standards. Our culture communicates the opposite message to young people. A common view today is that sex is to be expected as a normal part of growing up. God calls this a "great folly" (Prov. 5:23). Guard against the lie that sexual exploration is a rite of passage for young people. Call your child to sexual self-control; this is God's expectation for his or her life.

God has given you Proverbs 5 as a road map to use in talking with your child about sex. He has given you many passages in the Bible on the topic of sex. Read and discuss these with your child. Let his words be your words. Let his methods be your methods. Let his Spirit do the heavy lifting. Your responsibility is to share God's truth, point your child to Christ, and leave the results up to God.

Courageous Conversations

1. Read Proverbs 5:1–23 together. Invite your child to ask any questions that come to mind.
2. What does Proverbs 5:3–4 teach about sexual temptation? What do the words "honey" and "two-edged sword" tell us about temptation?
3. What three consequences might young people experience if they "do not ponder" the outcome of their sexual decisions?
   a. Proverbs 5:4
   b. Proverbs 5:5a
   c. Proverbs 5:5b
4. What encouragement does the father give his son in Proverbs 5:8? What application does this have for a young person today?
5. Sex outside marriage has a price tag. What four costs are mentioned in Proverbs 5:8–14?
   a. Proverbs 5:9
   b. Proverbs 5:9–10
   c. Proverbs 5:10
   d. Proverbs 5:11–13
6. In Proverbs 5:18–19, the father tells his son how to have a blessed, or happy, marriage. What two things does the father tell his son to do?
   a. Proverbs 5:18
   b. Proverbs 5:19
7. What does it mean to "rejoice" in a spouse and be "intoxicated with [his or her] love"? What application does this have for marriage?

8. What does the father/mother challenge the son/daughter to do with his or her sexual urges?
   - a. Proverbs 5:23. What causes death if it is lacking?
   - b. Titus 2:5a
   - c. Titus 2:6
9. What struggles and victories have you had with sexual self-control?
10. Some people suggest that having sex is a normal part of growing up. In the second line of Proverbs 5:23, what two words does God use to refer to sex outside marriage? What does this tell us about sexual experiences outside marriage?

Preparing Your Child for Purity

Three Biblical Methods to Implement

Have you considered that your child is going to have (or already does have) strong sexual urges? Like clockwork, sexual desires will develop in your child during his or her preteen years, and this happens even when parents filter the corrupting messages of the world. This chapter will help you prepare your child to stand firm against sexual temptation and to live in a way that is sexually pleasing to the Lord.

The Bible describes some common challenges that young people face during their teenage years that make sexual purity difficult. I encourage you to recognize the tendencies of youth and to intentionally prepare for them. Don't be the parent who overestimates your child's ability to say no to sin. Maybe your child is the most responsible, most godly, most amazing young person ever. Maybe your child has been blessed by God with the ability to control himself or herself in ways that few people can. You probably have an amazing child . . . but he or she is still a teenager.

God is realistic about adolescence, and you should be too. The Bible teaches the following things about this topic:

- *Young people need wisdom and often lack common sense.* The father in Proverbs regularly reminds his son to listen and points out that "I have perceived among the youths, a young man lacking sense" (Prov. 7:7). Your child may think that he or she knows it all, but he or she still needs your guidance.
- *Young people do not always choose the best company.* Again and again, the father in Proverbs warns his son to stay far away from seductive women and evil men. Proverbs 1:10 and 15 state, "My son, if sinners entice you, do not consent. . . . Do not walk in the way with them."
- *Young people need to be taught self-control.* In Titus 2, Paul instructs older men and women to teach younger men and women. What is the one thing that both young men and women need to learn? Self-control (see vv. 4, 6).

The combination of these tendencies means that *your child needs help staying sexually pure.* This isn't the time of life to grant total independence to a child. It is a time of life that requires a significant investment on the part of a parent. Preparing children for marriage is not only what a parent teaches in the early years but also how a parent encourages a child to pursue holiness in the later years. In this chapter and the next, we will look at what you can do to prepare your child to stand firm against sexual temptation and to live in a way that is sexually pure and pleasing to the Lord.

What Is Sexual Purity?

First Thessalonians 4:3–5 is the passage I like to turn to when I talk to young people about sexual purity.

> For this is the will of God, your sanctification: that you abstain from sexual immorality; that each one of you know how to control his own body in holiness and honor, not in the passion of lust like Gentiles who do not know God.

Here are a few key points from 1 Thessalonians 4:3–5:

- Sanctification, one's growth into the likeness of Christ, is closely connected to sexual purity. Your child cannot grow as a Christian and pursue sexual sin at the same time.
- God expects young people to control their sexual urges, not to give themselves over to them like individuals who do not know Jesus Christ. One of the things that makes Christians different from the world is our high sexual ethics.
- Sexual purity is the result of love for God and love for others, which Paul describes as holiness and honor.

Holiness is a big deal to God. It is central to his nature, and to be holy is a repeated command in Scripture. God instructs believers, "Be holy because I am holy" (1 Peter 1:16). Holiness means being "set apart." It means to be different or unique. It is the absence of any blemish or sin.

Purity is at the heart of holiness. Elisabeth Elliot, author of an excellent book on purity and the wife of missionary Jim Elliot, defines purity as "freedom from contamination, from anything that would spoil the taste or the pleasure, reduce the power, or in any way adulterate what the thing was meant to be."[1] Listen to what Elisabeth Elliot wrote about her own battle for sexual purity:

> As I grew into womanhood and began to learn what was in my heart I saw very clearly that, of all things difficult to rule, none were more so than my will and affections. They were unruly in the extreme. . . .
>
> Bringing anything at all into order . . . involves some expenditure. Time and energy at least are required. Perhaps even labor, toil, sacrifice, and pain.[2]

1. Elisabeth Elliot, *Passion and Purity: Learning to Bring Your Love Life Under Christ's Control* (Grand Rapids: Revell, 2002), 131–32.
2. Ibid., 34.

Elisabeth's experience echoes Jeremiah 17:9, which tells us that the heart is desperately sick and, as a result, desires all the wrong things. Sexual purity is no stroll through the park. It's toil. It's labor. Elisabeth recognized that it is hard work and that there was a cost to bringing her affections under the lordship of Christ. Yet, as a young person, Elisabeth was willing to labor and sacrifice in order to pursue personal holiness. She understood that sin is offensive to God. She knew that joy is found in obedience, not indulgence. She recognized that God has standards and that those standards aren't optional. She wanted to put off sexual sin and put on righteousness.

Our children need continual encouragement to do the same, as this is not their natural inclination. I hope that the Bible's caricature of adolescence reminds you to be a parent with presence; you cannot take a hands-off approach during your child's teen years. Do not underestimate the sexual battle that your child will face. Unruly sexual affections are the norm, not the exception, and God's standards are high.

Here are three ways you can help your child to maintain sexual purity.

Keep Your Child's Eyes on Christ

If your child is going to stand against the allure of sexual impurity, you can't simply tell him or her about all the negative consequences of premarital sex. Your child needs help in order to think theologically about sex and to submit his or her sexual practices to the Lord. To do that, *you need to dazzle your child with the all-satisfying beauty of Christ.*

Don't start with rules and regulations, boundaries, and consequences. Start with Christ. Tell of the wonders he has done. Talk about his nature. Point out his grandeur. Share what he has done in your life. Paint the picture of a glorious God who is so big, so amazing, so attractive that sexual immorality is seen as a cheap alternative.

A heart that is captivated by Christ won't be captured by a

170

God-replacement such as sex. When Jesus is small, sex can reign supreme. When Jesus is grand, glorious, and amazing to your child, sexual pleasure will not become an idol. When the Son is the center of your child's universe, the gravitational pull of sexual immorality will be weakened considerably.

What's going to make the difference for your son when an attractive girl walks by and a sexual thought pops into his head? What's going to make the difference for your daughter when she finds herself alone with her boyfriend—the one she is feeling very attracted to at the moment? What's going to make the difference when your child is engaged to be married and culture tells him or her that, because he or she is in a committed, monogamous relationship, the next step is to start living as if he or she is married?

Previous generations of parents tried to use external regulations to control behavior: Boundaries. Rings. Pledges. God has given us his law to be obeyed, and even delighted in—but when rules are emphasized apart from the gospel, they never work. If all we do is provide young people with rules, we provide them with two equally bad options. The first is to reject God's rules and live in rebellion. The second is to live believing that God's good favor has to be earned. A child ends up looking like either the woman at the well, who had no regard for marriage, or a legalistic Pharisee.

A purity ring or abstinence pledge, as helpful as it may be, won't make a difference when your child's passions are out of order, so don't start there. Start with Jesus. Dazzle your child with Christ and then encourage your child to obey the Lord. Your goal is to combine love and limits—to give your child law and gospel, not just rules and regulations.

Saturate Your Child's Mind with God's Word

"How can a young man keep his way pure?" asks the psalmist in Psalm 119:9. Here is his answer: "By guarding it according to your word. . . . I have stored up your word in my heart, that I might not sin against you." The psalmist, likely a young man, wants to do what is right. He desires to obey God. And in order to do that, he looks for methods. He wants tools. He asks, *how* can I stay pure?

This is the million-dollar question, and God has a time-tested answer. It sounds cliché, but the remedy that God provides for sexual sin is simple: Young people are to read his Word, meditate on his Word, and memorize his Word. God's Word is to fill their minds and hearts. Scripture is a young person's guard against sin. It's God's method of shielding the mind from impure thoughts and actions. A mind that is filled with God's Word and is meditating on his ways is less likely to be full of lustful thoughts and dreams of sexual fantasies.

It is not enough for us to encourage our children to be sexually pure; we need to put tools in their hands in order to help them succeed.[3] One of the best things you can do for your child's sexual purity is to encourage him or her to be in God's Word daily. You can do this by training your child to develop the spiritual habits of studying the Bible and memorizing Scripture.[4] Show your child how you study the Bible. He or she will gain much from your example. From time to time, ask your child what he or she is reading and learning. Your child will gain much from your accountability.

Here are three simple methods you can use to aid your child in Bible memorization.

- *Place key Scriptures strategically around the house for your child to see.* My wife and I sometimes write verses on a whiteboard or a chalkboard that apply to something our family has experienced or to a topic that one of our children is pondering.
- *Enroll your child in a Bible memorization program.* Most

3. A helpful tool is my eBook *6 Ways to Help Children Live According to God's Word*, available at https://www.RootedKids.com/product/6-ways-to-help-children-live-according-to-gods-word/.

4. Kay Arthur and Janna Arndt have written one of the more accessible books for young people on this subject, *How to Study Your Bible for Kids* (Eugene, OR: Harvest House, 2001). For older teens, John MacArthur's book *How to Study the Bible* (Chicago: Moody, 2009), is a good resource.

children's ministries and some youth ministries have some form of Bible memorization built into them. If your church has this available, I encourage you to use this tool. Our church uses Awana, which has some excellent Bible memorization tools. You can also create your own list of verses to memorize. You can find a list of my top twenty verses for young people using the Bible memorization tool called Rootworks at https://www.RootedKids.com/product/rootworks/.

- *Play music at home or in the car that sets Bible verses to song.* Children of all ages, and even adults, use this method to memorize Scripture, and there is a growing number of great resources available. Two of my favorites are Seeds Family Worship and Roots Kids Worship.[5]

There is a strong connection between the power of God's Word and personal holiness—a direct correlation between learning the Scriptures and living in a way that is pleasing to God. We should not be surprised if our children struggle with sexual purity when they are not in God's Word. Therefore, encourage your child to be saturated with the Word of God daily.

Set Boundaries for Your Child

Finally, although we don't start with rules and regulations, boundaries are necessary. You need to help your child to set and enforce sexual boundaries, especially when he or she is dating. Your child lives in a hypersexualized, do-what-you-wish world. Boundaries please God and reflect his desire for holiness, protect us from sin and its consequences, build trust, and honor others. I have never met a husband and wife who regret the boundaries that they made while dating. I have met plenty of couples who wish they had made more.

5. Roots Kids Worship can be found at https://rootedkids.com/product -category/music/?product_view=list.

Boundaries are about drawing lines. Why should our children place themselves in a situation in which they will face temptation? Why take the risk? This is the wisdom of Proverbs 6:27. The father asks his son, "Can a man scoop fire into his lap without his clothes being burned?" Of course the answer is no.

Proverbs 7:13–23 provides an example of what happens when boundaries are compromised. There is a snowball effect. Notice the progression: "She took hold of him and kissed him. . . . Come, let's drink deep of love till morning; let's enjoy ourselves with love! With persuasive words she led him astray. . . . All at once he followed her like an ox going to the slaughter."

From this passage, I think we can say that there is no such thing as a careless kiss. For this young person, making out led to making love. What he thought was one harmless kiss led to a one-night stand. Boundaries are a God-given line of defense against sexual sin.

Work with your child to establish boundaries. What does God want from your child physically as a single person? What safeguards should be considered in order to help your child remain sexually pure before marriage? What boundaries need to be put in place in order to support this effort?

In the evangelical community, there is a spectrum of opinions about what is physically acceptable and what is not during the dating days. I will leave the specifics up to each family to decide—but I want to provide some questions for a parent and child to discuss that may help toward that end.

- What safeguard needs to be put in place so that you "honor God with your body" (1 Cor. 6:20)?
- What boundaries should you consider so that there is not even "a hint" of sexual impurity in what you do (Eph. 5:3)?
- What lines need to be drawn so that you can say, after a date is over, that everything was done "in all purity" (1 Tim. 5:2)?
- What limits should you have in place so that, if others observed you on a date, God would be glorified in their eyes (see 1 Cor. 10:31)?

- What things would you be ashamed to tell your future husband or wife that you did with another man or woman (see Prov. 5:9–10)?

What I see in Scripture is that no standard of purity is too high. When I am working with young people, it is not uncommon for me to be asked, "How far is too far?" That is the wrong question to ask. When I read between the lines of this question, I'm hearing, "How close to the sexual line can I get without crossing it?" We are not to approach the line, but to flee from it (see 2 Tim. 2:22). The Bible encourages us to pursue godliness, and this goal should help us define boundaries. The following story illustrates this point well.

The Story of a Queen, Three Strong Men, and a Cliff

There once was a queen who lived at the top of a very tall, steep mountain. The path down from her castle was wide enough for a cart to comfortably travel up and down, but there were deadly cliffs on both sides of the path.

The queen decided to hire a strong man to pull her cart. Three well-built men applied for the job, each one with bulging muscles. The queen had no doubt that all three men could physically do the job at hand, so in the interview she asked but one question: "How close to the edge of the cliff do you believe you can safely navigate without falling?"

The first man confidently answered, "I can come within one foot of the edge without any problems."

The second strong man responded, "I can come within six inches of the edge and still face no danger."

The third strong man thought for a moment and then replied, "I will stay as far from the edge as possible, for I do not wish to endanger the life of the queen."

Who do you think the queen hired? The first two men believed that they could get close to the edge without any problem. The third man, the queen's choice, wanted to stay far away from danger.

When it comes to sexual purity, we want our children to have the same mind-set as the third man. Our children should not ask, "How far can I go physically without falling off the edge?" The motive behind this question is concerning. Rather than asking how far is too far, our children should ask what is required in order to live a life that is pleasing to God.

What boundaries should you consider? Here is an example from Pastor Matt Chandler.

> One of the things I say at The Village, on repeat, is that nothing good has ever come from a boyfriend and girlfriend cuddling on the couch watching a movie from 11pm to 1am. It has never ended in a discussion about cinematography in the history of watching movies on couches. To put yourself in that position to begin with is a foolish one.
>
> What works is being in public, guarding space alone, not putting yourself in situations. I think singles have a tendency to think more highly of their own self-control than they should. So, I think dating in groups, or dating in public, is important, and we see that in Scripture. In Song of Solomon you see a growing desire to be physically intimate, and yet she describes their date as being under this canopy of leaves and this rug of grass (Song 1:16–17). They are outside. They are at a park. They are in a forest. They are in the public eye, because they have a growing passion to be intimate physically. And yet, it is clear that they don't want to awaken love before it is time (Song 2:7; 3:5; 8:4). And so, they have positioned themselves publicly so as to not give themselves over to their lusts.[6]

This is sound wisdom. It is an example of boundaries that parents should encourage a child to pursue. When I was dating, my parents did not allow me to have any girl other than my sister in

6. Tony Reinke, "10 Questions on Dating with Matt Chandler," Desiring God, February 14, 2015, http://www.desiringgod.org/articles/10-questions-on-dating-with-matt-chandler.

my bedroom. They knew that nothing good comes from individuals being alone in a room.

For most people, physical touch and romantic kissing initiate a God-designed process that prepares them for sex. God created our bodies in this way. Sex begins with sexual activity. Kissing and touching are the on-ramp to that highway. Kissing is to sex what lightning is to thunder: one typically follows the other. Romantic physical activity is meant to lead to consummation, and the body knows this. Romantic physical activity is often the first step that an individual takes toward indulging in sexual sin. Boundaries need to take this into account.

What if you are discussing boundaries with your child and you get the response, "It's just kissing!"? Ask your child if it is possible to participate in a specific physical activity, such as kissing, and to obey God's biblical standard of holiness while doing it. The same question can apply to holding hands, giving a back rub, or any other type of physical touch in a dating relationship. Remember, the goal is holiness. If a physical activity leads to impure thoughts or actions, then it should be avoided.

God's desire is for our lives to be holy as he is holy. Until your child is married, your child should not live as if he or she is married. Children need to put boundaries in place that reflect God's desire for godliness.

G. K. Chesterton once said, "God gives us rules so that good things can run wild."[7] Let that sink in for a moment. Some people see boundaries as restrictive. For many people, Christianity is known only as a system of restraints. Chesterton helps us to consider *why* restrictions are a good thing. I encourage you to ask your child what good things can happen because of boundaries. God did not give us rules in order to steal our happiness and ruin our lives. He gave us limitations because he knew they would lead to an abundant life.

The last thing I will say on boundaries is that *they need to be made public.* A young person should let his or her parents know what

7. See G. K. Chesterton, *Orthodoxy* (1908; repr., Chicago: Moody, 2009), 144.

kind of person he or she is striving to be. Toward the beginning of a relationship, your child should clarify his or her sexual standards to the person whom he or she is dating. This will allow others to reinforce the perimeter that a young person is setting. It's a built-in accountability tool. And the more people we have to hold our children accountable, the less likely our children will be to go out of bounds sexually.

Courageous Conversations

1. Read 1 Thessalonians 4:3–5.
   a. What two things does this passage teach that God expects from us sexually?
   b. How is a young person's spiritual growth connected to his or her sexual obedience?
2. Read 1 Peter 1:16. What is holiness? Why is it a big deal to God?
3. Read Psalm 119:9–11. What three things does this passage instruct a young person to do in order to remain sexually pure?
4. Evaluate yourself. How are you doing with reading and memorizing God's Word? If these are not consistent habits of yours, what changes should you make in order to enable you to develop these spiritual disciplines?
5. Parent, show your child how you study the Bible. What tools can your child use to read and memorize God's Word? How could a commentary, concordance, or study Bible be useful toward these ends?
6. As parent and child, consider together what boundaries to put in place, read the following passages, and answer the accompanying questions.
   a. When you are dating, what safeguards should you put in place so that you "honor God with your body" (1 Cor. 6:20)?
   b. What boundaries do you need to consider so that there is not even "a hint" of sexual impurity in what you do (Eph. 5:3)?

    c. What lines need to be drawn so that you can say, after a date is over, that everything was done "in all purity" (1 Tim. 5:2)?

    d. What limits should you have in place so that, if others observed you on a date, God would be glorified in their eyes (see 1 Cor. 10:31)?

    e. What things would you be ashamed to tell your future husband or wife that you did with another man or woman (see Prov. 5:9–10)?

    f. What example are we provided in the Bible (see Song 4:12)?

7. What guidelines or boundaries should be put in place in order to help a young person maintain sexual purity? Discuss the following questions so there are shared expectations prior to a child's dating days.

    a. Should dating occur in groups, alone, or some of both?

    b. Generally, what time of night should a young person be home?

    c. What are good activities and unwise activities to do on a date?

    d. What forms of physical touch are acceptable (holding hands, hugging, kissing, and so on)?

    e. Is it desirable for a father to interview his daughter's date?

    f. What other boundaries should be considered?

8. Read the story of the queen and the three strong men found on page 175.

    a. What can we learn from this story about boundaries?

    b. What is the problem with asking, "How close to the edge can I get sexually?"

    c. In Proverbs 6:27, a father asks his son, "Can a man scoop fire into his lap without his clothes being burned?" How would you answer this question? What can a young person learn from this warning as it relates to boundaries in dating?

    d. Read Proverbs 7:12–23 and note the physical progression that takes place. What started the snowball effect? What can we learn from this example?

9. Read Song of Songs 8:8–9. What two metaphors does the author use to talk about sexual purity? What does a wall signify? What does a door suggest? If this young person is not able to withstand sexual temptation on his or her own, what steps do family members take in the second half of verse 9? What application regarding boundaries can be made from this passage?

10. Work together to make a list of boundaries that parent and child agree on.

14

TALKING TO YOUR CHILD
ABOUT PORNOGRAPHY
AND LUST

Three Ways to Help Your
Child Strive for Holiness

Don and Callie were horrified when they heard the news. Their third-grade son had been exposed to pornography while doing homework on school computers, as well as from a classmate who watched it freely at home and then discussed it in great detail with classmates. At the tender age of eight, Erik had an experience that is all too common today. He had seen a distorted picture of sex.

A different parent caught his nine-year-old daughter looking at porn on her iPad. A sixth-grade student from her bus had left a handout from her health class on the bus seat; his daughter had seen the handout, picked it up, and become curious. Rather than ask her parents, she had turned to the Internet for answers. From her perspective, the Internet wouldn't get angry at her like a parent might or make fun of her like a friend might. As a result of her curiosity, this nine-year-old girl discovered porn.

There are more children looking at pornography, at younger

ages and with greater frequency, than ever before. I receive calls and emails regularly from parents whose children have stumbled upon porn by accident or pursued it with intention. Parents need to do some preventative and preparatory work with children in this area.

Porn is as addictive as a drug and carries a heavy cost. Viewing pornography ruins relationships and impacts beliefs. If your child gets caught in the porn trap, you can expect some or all of the following issues:

- Negative views of and aggression toward the opposite gender.
- Decreased interest in a godly relationship and a godly spouse.
- Increased likelihood of premarital sex, divorce, and unfaithfulness in marriage.
- Loss of trust from parents or a future spouse.
- Distorted pictures of sex and the view that promiscuity is normal.

It's not a matter of *if* our children will be exposed to porn but *when*.[1] Children are often first exposed to pornography when an Internet search pulls up a crude image. When they encounter porn, they should already know exactly what to do.

One way to talk about pornography with young people is to talk about modesty (see 1 Tim. 2:9). If you have a young child, this will allow you to talk about pornography without being explicit, as pornography is a form of immodesty.

Explain to your child that to be modest is to dress respectfully and in an ordered fashion. We are modest when we cover our body with clothes, but, more specifically, we are modest when we wear clothes that we would want others to wear if they were around us. Modesty is a way to love our neighbors. If your child asks you, "What is pornography?" tell him or her that it is when people get immodest, take pictures, and let other people see the pictures.

When modesty is the angle you take, it's an easy way to talk

---

1. A common age for first exposure is around nine or ten years old.

about purity and pornography without having to talk about the crude side of things. Tell your child that God does not want us to dress immodestly or to look at people who are dressed in an immodest way. This informs what clothes we buy, how we dress at home and in public, what we look at, and what we watch on TV. Train your child to walk away or look away when he or she encounters immodesty. If, for some reason, your child stumbles onto a pornographic site, he or she will know that it is immodest and will have been already trained how to respond.

In practical terms, you can help your child to successfully navigate cyberspace by doing the following:

- Pre-teaching your child what to do if a pornographic or impure image appears on the screen. Don't look. Don't linger. Close the page. Tell a parent or teacher.
- Placing an Internet filter on your computers and safeguarding your child's phone or tablet. A high percentage of porn is viewed on phones. Sadly, many parents provide children with these devices without safeguarding them and, in doing so, have given their children free and unlimited access to pornography.
- Paying attention to the apps, video games, social media sites, movies, and literature that your child is consuming. Children are regularly exposed to pornography through these avenues.

Pornography is so common that a section on purity would not be complete without addressing it. However, it is only one form of sexual impurity, which also includes sexual fantasies, masturbation, premarital sex, and homosexuality.

What Is Sexual Impurity?

Sexual impurity comes from lust. Lust is uncontrolled desire. It is a longing to have sex with someone whom the Bible forbids. I explain lust to children by saying that it is sexual desire for someone

183

you are not married to, and once again I turn to 1 Thessalonians 4:3–5.

> For this is the will of God, your sanctification: that you abstain from sexual immorality; that each one of you know how to control his own body in holiness and honor, not in the passion of lust like Gentiles who do not know God.

John Piper gets his definition of lust from 1 Thessalonians 4. He says that lust is "sexual desire that disregards God and dishonors others" and describes it in this way:

> Sexual desire in itself is good. God made it in the beginning. It has its proper place. But it was made to be governed or regulated or guided by two concerns: honor toward the other person and holiness toward God. Lust is what that sexual desire becomes when that honor and that holiness are missing from it.[2]

Lust is dishonoring because all that lust wants is to use another person for one's own personal pleasure. Lust does not care about the other person in the way that a husband is to care for a wife and vice versa. It is not concerned with serving or helping the other person. God created sexual desire as a servant of marriage for the purpose of bringing a husband and wife together. Without the context of marriage, sexual desire becomes a greedy grab for self-fulfillment at the cost of others and with a blind eye toward God. Lust disregards God because it ignores his commands regarding how and when sex is to be pursued. Ultimately, lust is the corruption of sexual desire.

We live in a society that *intentionally* fuels sexual desire, and this makes sexual purity a challenge. If your child claims that it is okay to look at porn, masturbate, or have sex outside marriage, you can take your child to 1 Thessalonians 4:3–5 and point out that God

---

2. John Piper, "Battling the Unbelief of Lust," Desiring God, November 13, 1988, http://www.desiringgod.org/messages/battling-the-unbelief-of-lust.

commands single people to abstain from sex and to control sexual desire.

Why does God want sexual purity for your child? Matthew 5:8 answers that question: "Blessed are the pure in heart, for they shall see God." The person who lives as sexually impure will limit his or her own intimacy with God. This reason alone should be enough to encourage a young person to establish boundaries that maintain sexual purity and help fight lustful sexual desires. The young person who zealously pursues sexual purity is promised the sight of God. That is a great promise!

How should your child respond to sexual desire? Here are three biblical methods.

Flee Youthful Passions

When young people have sexual desires, society encourages them to experiment, explore, and indulge. The Bible teaches the exact opposite. It tells young people to run from sexual temptation. Like Joseph, our children need to flee from sinful sexual offerings (see Gen. 39:11). Joseph removed himself from an impure situation and was victorious in maintaining his sexual purity. He is a great example worthy of imitation.

In addition to Joseph, we have the example of Timothy. Paul knew that sexual temptation would be a challenge for young Timothy, because he gave Timothy the following instruction: "So flee youthful passions and pursue righteousness, faith, love, and peace, along with those who call on the Lord from a pure heart" (2 Tim. 2:22). Like Timothy, our children need to fight the good fight of faith and set an example in purity (see 1 Tim. 4:12). Sexual purity will not come without a fight. Your child needs to be ready for a sexual battle.

What did Paul instruct Timothy to do when a sexual desire came into his mind? Paul instructed Timothy to flee. The term *flee* carries with it the idea of turning and running from something. One of God's defenses against sexual sin is our feet. Our children need to learn when to walk out of the movie, when to shut off the television, when to change the radio station, when to leave a room, and when they should literally run from a seductive person, leaving their coat in his or her hand. And they need to have the conviction to do it. Sexual sin is not something to flirt with.

Put to Death Ungodly Sexual Desire

Young people tend to rationalize the acceptability of sexual desire, minimize the sinfulness of lustful thoughts, and wonder why this issue is a big deal. They see ungodly sexual desire as a small sin compared to the other sexual sins of the Bible. It is important to address the mind-set that it is okay to fantasize sexually as long as the thoughts are not acted upon. This mind-set fails to recognize that entertaining sexual desire is the first step toward engaging in sexual practice. If your child thinks sexual thoughts, eventually he or she will act on them.

The Bible calls your child to have a *lust-fighting faith*. Here are a few examples.

- "Take captive every thought to make it obedient to Christ" (2 Cor. 10:5 NIV).
- "Whatever is true, whatever is honorable, whatever is just, whatever is pure, whatever is lovely, whatever is commendable, if there is any excellence, if there is anything worthy of praise, think about these things" (Phil. 4:8).
- "On my bed I remember [God]; I think of you through the watches of the night" (Ps. 63:6 NIV).

Romans 8:13 tells young people exactly what to do with ungodly sexual desire. It is radical: "By the Spirit you put to death the deeds of the body." What is God's answer for ungodly sexual desire? Kill it. Put it to death. Give it no chance to take root in your child's heart or life.

Be sure to emphasize Romans 8:13 with your child. Our children are to bring all their sexual desires under the lordship of Christ.

186

It isn't enough to focus on sexual practice; you have to go deeper than that. You have to get to the heart and to what is happening in the mind of your child. Jesus states, "'You shall not commit adultery.' But I say to you that everyone who looks at a woman with lustful intent has already committed adultery with her in his heart" (Matthew 5:27–28). Jesus equates sexual fantasies in the heart with sexual practice in the body. In God's eyes, they are one and the same. The sin of lustful thought is as serious as the sin of adultery.

The Bible is clear: *sexual purity starts in the mind.* External boundaries aren't enough. In fact, if we focus all our energy there, we have already lost the battle. Internal boundaries are also needed. The Bible teaches that boundaries begin in our hearts and extend out from there.

God is concerned about what is happening in your child's mind, and you should be as well. Wandering eyes and second glances are a big deal—pay attention to them! Safeguard your home so that you are not putting images before your child that feed an ungodly thought life. If your child struggles in this area, take action.

Jesus has some radical advice when it comes to your child's sexual purity: "If your right eye causes you to sin, tear it out and throw it away. For it is better that you lose one of your members than that your whole body be thrown into hell" (Matt. 5:29). This passage emphasizes the seriousness of sin and the importance of holiness. Sin is not to be entertained. It is to be eliminated. Do whatever is necessary to help your child put to death sexual sin in his or her life. Matthew 5:29 encourages you to take decisive and radical action if necessary.

Remember, every thought and action is done in full view of God. Proverbs 5:2 states, "For a man's ways are in full view of the Lord, and he examines all his paths." With God, there is no such thing as a secret sin. He knows all and sees all, and that should motivate your child to walk in paths of righteousness.

Make a Job 31:1 Covenant

One of my favorite passages for young people on sexual purity is Job 31:1: "I made a covenant with my eyes not to look lustfully

187

at a woman." Read this passage to your child and remind your child that lust is a sin. Rather than give in to ungodly sexual desire, Job made a promise to himself that he would not look at a woman and desire to have sex with her. You can teach your child to have the same conviction.

Give your child the Job 31:1 challenge. Challenge your child to imitate Job, who did not look lustfully at others. Job made a resolution not to think about a woman in an impure way. He imposed a restriction upon himself, and this aided his effort to maintain a pure heart. Job refused to indulge in unholy desires. He did not allow himself to dwell on impure longings nor to be polluted by ungodly images. Such a person is worthy of emulation.

A young person who wishes to maintain sexual purity must make this promise to himself or herself and to God—a promise so sincere, so sacred, so firm that he or she will not entertain for a moment an impure sexual desire. When an impure image comes before your child, whether in print, in digital format, or in person, your child will have the wisdom to recognize the danger and the internal conviction to guard his or her eyes and look away. As a result, the young person will instinctively alter his or her gaze or walk away. The Job 31:1 covenant trains children to think about what is pure, honorable, lovely, and commendable rather than what is not (see Phil. 4:8).

In Pursuit of Happiness

Your child is on a quest for happiness. American culture is trying to convince your child that happiness is found in sexual pleasure. You need to help your child develop the conviction that happiness is found by obeying God's commands. Obedience always leads to joy.

Elisabeth Elliot writes, "When obedience to God contradicts what I think will give me pleasure, let me ask myself if I love Him. If I can say yes to that question, can't I say yes to pleasing Him?"[3] She

---

3. Elisabeth Elliot, *Passion and Purity: Learning to Bring Your Love Life Under Christ's Control* (Grand Rapids: Revell, 2002), 90.

concludes, "Yes to God *always* leads in the end to joy."[4] What a great reminder for children to hear.

God's commands are to govern a young person's sexual choices. Absolute purity is expected in the Bible. Sexual practices are not a matter of individual appetite. As such, we must ensure that our children do not make the error of interpreting the Bible through the lens of sexuality but rather interpret their sexuality through the lens of the Bible. Your child must have the deep-down conviction that sexual impurity is not good. Every child must decide whether he or she loves sin more than the Lord. As our children ponder their paths, let us always keep a great promise of Scripture before them: "Blessed are the pure in heart, for they shall see God" (Matt. 5:8).

Courageous Conversations

1. Read 1 Timothy 2:9. What is modesty?
    a. What does it mean to dress modestly?
    b. Evaluate the clothes you wear. Are they modest or immodest?
    c. What should you do if you see an immodestly dressed person on the computer, on television, or in person?
2. According to 1 Thessalonians 4:3–5, what is lust?
3. Read Matthew 5:8. What does "pure in heart" mean? What is the promise given to those who are pure in heart? On the flip side, what does that mean for the person who harbors lust or pursues sexual sin?
4. What defense does the Bible provide for young people against sexual sin? Read the following verses:
    a. 2 Timothy 2:22
    b. Genesis 39:11
    c. 1 Timothy 4:12
5. Rather than explore or indulge in sexual sin, what do the following verses instruct young people to do with ungodly sexual desire?

4. Ibid.

       a. Romans 8:13

       b. Colossians 3:5

       c. 2 Corinthians 10:5

       d. Philippians 4:8

       e. Psalm 63:6

6. Read Matthew 5:27–29. What does Jesus equate lust to? What does this passage teach us about sexual sin? What steps does Jesus want us to take in order to avoid sexual sin? Is there anything you need to change or remove from your life in order to live in a pleasing manner before God?

7. Read Proverbs 5:21. What does this passage remind us?

8. Read Job 31:1 and give your child the Job 31:1 challenge. What promise did Job make to himself? What can we learn from Job's example?

15

ARE CRUSHES OKAY?

Responding to Attraction
in a Way That Honors God

You remember your first crush, right?[1] Do you remember how old you were when it happened? Third grade? Fourth? Maybe you were a late bloomer and didn't experience a crush until fifth or sixth grade. Usually, children begin to notice the opposite gender sometime around their mid to late elementary years. The way that girls interact with boys changes. Instead of running with them, they start to run away from them. Girls who were completely uninterested in how they dressed suddenly care. Boys start to pick on girls as a sign of affection.

I noticed this when I taught K–8 physical education at a small Christian school in the inner city. As I was teaching, I watched students transform during their fourth-grade year. When they entered PE as new fourth graders, they dressed like children and still wore clothes with dinosaurs and daisies on them. Children of both genders mingled with one another in class. The kids didn't care about bedhead or the remnant of lunch on their faces. But around January 1, the girls started dressing differently, talking differently, and interacting differently with the boys. Huddles of girls began to form. The dreaded whispering

---

1. A crush is a strong physical attraction to another person and the beginning of a God-designed process that leads toward marriage.

191

began, with glances to the boys and then giggles. For months, most of the boys were oblivious to this. After all, perception has never been a strong suit for most guys.

But then, toward the end of the school year, the early blooming boys began to see girls differently. Their clothes, tastes, and interactions began to be noticeably different. And then the crushes began. Girls would send scouts to find out what Jimmy thought of Jackie. Boys, too shy to talk with girls, would send notes. Sometimes students who were unsure about their newfound feelings would confide in me as they were jumping rope or dribbling a basketball.

I remember one question, as clear as day: "Is it okay to have a crush on a girl?" And there it was—the phenomenon that was sweeping through the fourth-grade class like a tsunami. I was surprised that nine- and ten-year-olds were already becoming romantically interested in one another. I'd thought it was more of a middle school thing. But it was happening right in front of my eyes.

This was not an isolated experience. When I was a middle school pastor, an incoming sixth grader asked me, "Is it wrong to have a crush?" This student was noticeably troubled about his warm, fuzzy feelings over girls. He liked them. He thought they were cute. And he felt that might not be pleasing to God. He didn't know how to handle his feelings in a way that honored God.

If your child asks you, "Is it okay to be physically attracted to others?" how will you answer? At around ten years of age, your child may not verbalize this question, but he or she will be thinking about it.

Here are three things to talk with your child about.

Crushes Are Normal

Physical attraction is a normal part of growing up. It is the first step in a natural progression toward marriage. Plenty of children have been caught off guard by unexpected warm fuzzies and have begun to think that something is wrong with them. It's helpful, when you are ten years old, to know that you are not going to grow a tail or start howling at the moon.

The first thing we should do as parents is to explain what will happen. We should let our children know that, in the future, the opposite gender will start to look attractive. At some point, they will stop seeing cooties and start seeing cuties. When this happens, it is normal. These feelings are not wrong or sinful. It is good for our children to know this before such feelings arrive.[2]

I have celebrated this progression with my children, not shied away from it. I have told them it is a sign that they are growing into a man or a woman and that God is starting to prepare their hearts and bodies for marriage. It's opened the door to good conversations and some good laughs. The conversations become critical teaching opportunities to help young people learn to evaluate who is worth pursuing in the future and who is not. If Proverbs teaches us anything about adolescent individuals, it's that they often desire the wrong thing. Knowing the types of individuals whom our children find attractive enables parents to guide a child's affection toward individuals who love Jesus and are inwardly beautiful.

A Crush Is a Craving for Marriage

A crush is a heart-deep craving for marriage. Why is that? Because a crush is only a phase. By design, it's a short phase. It operates as the temporary glue that gives a person time to evaluate someone's character. Eventually, feelings fade and butterflies disappear. That's why physical attraction can ignite, but never sustain, a relationship. Physical attraction is meant to move a couple to a deeper kind of love. That deeper love is meant to culminate in a marriage covenant. Infatuation is meant to diminish so that lasting love can grow.

Help your child to understand that being physically attracted to

---

2. If your child experiences same-sex attraction, then it is helpful to recognize that this is a disordered desire according to the Bible and one that fits into the category of temptation. As with any temptation, the Christian is told to flee from sin and to fiercely fight for obedience to God. Experiencing same-sex attraction is not sin if the desire is put to death before it becomes lustful thoughts. Help your child by encouraging him or her to turn to Christ and trust God's promises.

another person is the thirst-inducing salt for marriage that God has hardwired into his or her biological development. A childhood crush points to the biblical truth that marriage is God's expected norm for people. It is God who created humans with the desire to love and be loved. He designed humans with a biological clock that puts marriage on the minds of youngsters at a ripe young age. If it is not good for man to be alone, then it makes sense that God would instill the innate desire within us for marriage.

Proverbs 20:5 states, "The purpose in a man's heart is like deep water, but a man of understanding will draw it out." Parents, you are the man of understanding for your child. Your son probably won't understand why he thinks girls are cute all of a sudden. Your daughter may be confused by her intense desire to spend every waking moment with a guy. You can let your child know that this is a shadow of a deeper desire that God has instilled in his or her heart for marriage.

Crushes Are Feelings

Feelings make good servants but poor masters. Feelings are meant to inform us that something is happening in our heart; they are *not* meant to be blindly acted on. Young people need to be warned not to become intoxicated with infatuation. They need to be reminded that feelings, even strong feelings, do not equal love.

Sadly, society feeds our children different advice. *Follow your heart* is some of the worst advice a child can ever receive, especially when applied to dating and marriage. A popular saying captures this cultural value: "If it feels so right, how can it be so wrong?" It's wrong because feelings aren't the authority on what is right, good, or true. Children need to be trained to base decisions *not* on feelings but on the timeless truths of God's Word. The Bible teaches that the heart is desperately wicked and a fountain of evil (see Jer. 17:9). Is this what we want to teach our children to follow?

When children begin to have feelings for someone else, these feelings need to be run through the grid of God's Word and the godly counsel of their parents. Sometimes, feelings blind children to the truth. Nothing interferes with common sense more than hormones do. That is why our children need to believe wholeheartedly the truth of Proverbs 3:5: "Trust in the Lord with all your heart and lean not on your own understanding." The appeal that we make to our children is that they trust God, not their feelings or perceived knowledge. God's ways are always the best ways. Those who follow them will be blessed.

There is nothing inherently wrong with a child having a crush. A crush becomes sinful when it leads to fantasizing thoughts or compromising actions. It can be exhilarating to feel as though the world revolves around another person. The problem is, the only person who is worthy of our child's first and greatest affection is Jesus. Anyone else becomes an idol.

How can you help your child to guard against an attraction that becomes the doorway to fantasizing thoughts or idolatrous affections? By doing everything you can to ensure that your child has a vision for the greatness of God. Children whose God is big and sovereign—a God who works miracles and raises the dead, a God who created the world simply by speaking and who sits on his throne as King—won't be captivated by one of God's creations. Children who have a small God have a big need to find someone else who appears larger than life. Help your child to be captivated by his or her Creator in order to avoid capture by one of God's attractive creations.

Courageous Conversations

1. What does it mean to have a crush on somebody?
2. Have you ever thought that someone was cute or attractive? If so, what did you find attractive about them?
3. Why do you think God created other people to look attractive to us? What is God's purpose for physical attraction?
4. What should you do if you have a crush?
5. When does physical attraction become sinful?
6. What is wrong with the advice to "just follow your heart"? What advice does Proverbs 3:5–6 provide?

◆◆◆ PART 4 ◆◆◆

DATING

16

WHAT IS THE
PURPOSE OF DATING?

Dating Is a Method—with a Goal

Ethan, a brand-new sixth grader, thrust a haphazardly folded piece of paper into my hands, turned red in the face, and asked if I could answer some things he was thinking about. Then he stood awkwardly while he waited for me to unfold the paper and read his questions.

A quick glance at it revealed a dozen questions surrounding the topic of dating and marriage. The first question on the paper, the one at the top of the page, the one that this student was thinking most about, was this: "What is the purpose of dating?"

That's a great question. I've asked this many times in one-on-one meetings and to large groups of students. I've learned never to assume that a young person approaches dating from a biblical perspective. For most young people, dating is what everyone does. That's what they see on TV, hear about in songs, and are conditioned to pursue at early ages.

Every young person has a reason for dating. As parents, we want their reason to be the right reason. Your job is to do some diagnostic work to figure out what is at the heart of your child's desire to date. I suggest that you ask two questions:

1. What do you believe is the purpose of dating?
2. Why do you want to date?

From young people's responses to these questions, I have encountered five different views on dating:

- *Dating? Yuck!* This is often the response from young people who are embarrassed to talk about the subject or who insist that they will be single forever. Their view of marriage is *poor.*
- *Dating is potentially harmful.* In this view, courting is the only acceptable means of pursuing a future husband or wife. Casual dating, as it takes place commonly in the United States, places young people in compromising situations that are often filled with sexual temptations. The dating and breaking up cycle desensitizes young people to commitment and is training them for future divorce. Dating is viewed as *problematic.*
- *Dating is fun.* Young people want a good time. They are looking for intimacy; they want to spend time with friends. Dating is new and exciting. It may increase their popularity. Marriage is not on the forefront of their mind. The driving motive is *pleasure.*
- *Dating will prepare for marriage.* Young people use dating to help them learn who they are and what they are looking for in a future spouse. It is seen as a practice ground for marriage. Dating is used as a means to *prepare* a young person for successful future relationships.
- *Dating will help to discover a spouse.* The main purpose for dating is to confirm whether a date is the one whom a young person plans to marry. Dating is unnecessary unless marriage is in the near future. There is intentional *purpose* to dating.

From among these five views, why does your child want to date? The most common reason that I hear from young people is some version of number three. Marriage may be in the back of their minds as they date recreationally, but it is so distant that there is a disconnect between dating and marriage. And that is a problem. In fact, it's a dating dilemma.

A Biblical Vision of Dating

When you approach this subject with your child, start by asking him or her to come up with a definition for dating. Allow your child to wrestle with the definition for a while and then discuss it. Your child may respond in one of the following ways:

- Dating is being in an exclusive relationship.
- Dating is having no desire to be with anyone else.
- Dating is having a boyfriend or a girlfriend.[1]

Young people need a vision for dating that is based on the Bible. The challenge, of course, is that the word *dating* isn't found in Scripture. In Bible times, and throughout much of history, marriages were arranged. Dating didn't exist. Neither did courting.

Here are the methods that I see described in Scripture:

- Parents choose a spouse for their children—for example, Abraham finds a wife for Isaac (see Gen. 24) and Saul gives Michal to David (see 1 Sam. 18).
- Ruth communicates her desire to marry Boaz at a co-ed sleepover (see Ruth 3).
- Single men from the tribe of Benjamin go to an annual festival, hide in the vineyards until the girls of Shiloh came out to dance, and then rush from the vineyards, each man catching and carrying off a young woman to be his wife (see Judges 21:15–23).

If you really want to stick to biblical methods, I just provided three options for you to choose from. I don't think that arranged

---

1. These are definitions I've heard from students.

marriages will return to prominence anytime soon, despite the wishes of many parents. Nor do I think the co-ed sleepover or sniper methods are options that most parents feel good about.

Like it or not, dating is the method that society has chosen as the primary way to find a spouse in the United States in the twenty-first century. Dating is simply the road to marriage, which is why you need to be clear on what the Bible has to say about marriage. Confusion about marriage leads to fogginess about dating. On the flip side, clarity about God's covenant of marriage provides parents with pinpoint precision regarding the purpose of dating, helps them to set boundaries, and answers situation-specific requests from children when they arise.

Don't get hung up on the method. Arranged marriages, courting, and dating are all methods that different cultures, at different times in history, have used to help young people arrive at marriage. Each of them has been used successfully to the glory of God as well as misused and abused. The issue isn't dating versus courting; it's why and how a person dates or courts.[2] Dating should be *a Christ-centered relationship between a man and a woman meant to help a couple discern marital compatibility with each other.*

When I look through the pages of the Bible, I don't see any evidence that recreational or preparatory dating is a good thing. I see the Bible treating engagement like marriage (e.g., in the case of Joseph and Mary). Broader than this, never once in the Bible do I see a romantic relationship between a man and a woman taken lightly. It is never a casual thing. Romantic relationships in the Bible are always taken seriously.

We should follow this tone in our guidance to young people. All dating is to be intentional dating with the end goal of marriage. If a young person is not ready to get married or a potential date is not marriage material, then there is no reason to date. We have to

---

2. If you prefer the courting method, great. I'll refer you to Joshua Harris's book *I Kissed Dating Goodbye: A New Attitude Toward Romance and Relationships* (Colorado Springs: Multnomah, 2003).

help our children understand that dating is not primarily for personal entertainment or character refinement. Enjoyment and growth will certainly be outcomes of dating, but they alone are insufficient reasons to enter into a dating relationship.

What is the purpose of dating? *Date to find your mate.* Use dating as the discerning process for marriage. The goal of dating is clarity. Its intention is marriage. Its danger is intimacy. Its requirement is being equally yoked. Marshall Segal explains this well: "While the great prize in marriage is Christ-centered intimacy, the great prize in dating is Christ-centered clarity. . . . The purpose of our dating is determining whether the two of us should get married, so we should focus our effort there."[3]

God's design for marriage speaks to his design for dating. We want to caution our children against entering into a dating relationship casually, carelessly, or quickly. Dating doesn't exist to provide a young person with someone to hang out with or make out with. Almost always, these dating arrangements leave somebody wounded. It's good to remind our children that their hearts weren't built to be borrowed.[4]

When Should a Young Person Begin Dating?

The Song of Songs encourages readers to refrain from pursuing romantic love until the time is right. Three times we are reminded "not to awaken love until the right time" (Song 2:7; 3:5; 8:4). It is important to recognize that if there is a right time, then there is also a wrong time to enter into a romantic relationship.

The word *awaken* literally means to arouse, stimulate, and stir. Solomon warns us not to intentionally stimulate or arouse love until it can be acted on. Does dating arouse love? In my experience, it

3. Marshall Segal, "When the Not-Yet Married Meet: Dating to Display Jesus," Desiring God, June 6, 2013, http://www.desiringgod.org/articles/when-the-not-yet-married-meet-dating-to-display-jesus.
4. See ibid.

does. Romantic dating has the potential to awaken a God-designed process that is meant to culminate in marriage. Dating, by nature, begins the process of two people becoming one emotionally, spiritually, and sometimes physically. Therefore, we can apply the wisdom in Solomon's charge to dating and *avoid early dating*.

When parents allow a child to date at a young age, they are encouraging an activity that has the strong potential to stimulate a child's mind and body in all the wrong ways. Self-control becomes very difficult for individuals who began dating too early. They have created urges for which there is no sexual outlet at this point in their lives. No wonder we have sexually charged teenagers walking around. Combine early dating with delayed marriage, and you have a ripe environment for sexual sin to occur.

How old should a young person be before dating? What is the right age to date? Thirteen, sixteen, eighteen, twenty-one, thirty years old? There is no hard-and-fast age requirement in the Bible. The Bible never explicitly says when a young person should or should not begin pursuing marriage.

When I was a youth pastor, I took a hard stance against dating during high school for any reason. Now I leave that door cautiously open. I think it is best for a young person to patiently wait until their post–high school years to date. I also think there are exceptions. God decides when he will introduce future spouses to each other. For some, this may be when they are teenagers.[5]

This is why the real issue isn't age, but maturity. Is a young person mature enough to handle the responsibility of dating? Is a young person at a point in life when he or she is ready to pursue marriage? There are a number of ways to look for the marks of maturity. The following is not an exhaustive list, but these criteria could be used to help determine the readiness of a child to pursue marriage:

5. This became clear to me a few years ago when I officiated four weddings of former students of mine. All four couples began dating during their high school years. Now when I talk to students, I like to tell them that their future husbands or wives might be sitting in the room with them right now.

- strong biblical convictions
- trustworthiness in other areas of life
- regular and open communication with parents
- godly treatment of the opposite-gendered parent and siblings
- understanding of the biblical meaning of marriage and the roles of a husband and wife

Your child will likely feel pressure to date. He or she may come to a point at which all his or her close friends are dating. That's okay. It doesn't mean that your son or daughter must follow that same path. Many adults have regrets about their dating days, often stemming from starting too early, being too casual about convictions, and not being intentional about the pursuit of a spouse. We should remember this when we think about our children dating.

Dating is serious business. If our children have the strong conviction that dating is designed for the pursuit of marriage, they will date accordingly. They will enter into a relationship intentionally. They will choose a date carefully. They will seek God's direction prayerfully.

Courageous Conversations

1. What is dating? Ask your child to come up with a definition.
2. Have you had any interest in dating someone? If so, tell me about it.
3. What do you believe is the purpose of dating?
4. What is a biblical reason to romantically pursue someone?
5. Read Song of Songs 8:4. What does this passage teach about when a young person should pursue a romantic relationship?
6. What is the danger of awakening love before a young person can act on those feelings?
7. According to Song of Songs 8:4, there is a "right time" to awaken love. That means there is also a "wrong time" to date. What are right and wrong times to date? Or, said another way, what are good and bad reasons to date?
8. What key marks of maturity should be present before a young person begins dating?

DATING AND PARENTS

Being a Wise Ally to Your Child

Young people often treat dating as if it is none of their parents' business. And many parents oblige, adopting a laissez-faire attitude and allowing their teenage children to pursue dating relationships with limited parental involvement. The problem is that parental passivity and teenage dating is rarely a good combination.

Parents have a critical role in the life of a teenage child who is dating. As parents, we want to help our children navigate one of life's most important decisions and do so in a way that honors God and helps the children themselves.

Before Your Child Starts Dating

Parents can do a number of things in anticipation of the day their child will date.

Pray

Begin praying for your child's future spouse as early and often as possible. If this isn't on your prayer list, add it.[1] In our family prayer

---

1. If you need a tool, Sylvia Gunter's book *For the Family* (Birmingham: The

times, Jen and I often pray out loud that our children will marry people who love Jesus and live for God. My older children have begun to internalize these prayers and now repeat them as their own when praying for their siblings and themselves.

Build and Maintain a Healthy Relationship with Your Child

It's not uncommon for parents to approach me, alarmed about who their children are dating or worried about their children's lack of communication, and to ask for help. I often start by asking, "Tell me about your relationship with your teenage child. Is it solid or struggling? Is it healthy or hurting?"

In chapter 3, I touched on the correlation between the quality of relationship a parent has with a child and the depth of impact that parent can have with him or her. We invite people to speak into our lives when we trust them and have a good relationship with them. If a parent and child are not on good terms, the child is unlikely to welcome the parent's advice or involvement. Establishing a healthy relationship with your child is critical in order to avoid limited communication or a rebellious spirit in the future.

Parents who are emotionally or physically distant during the early years of a child's life can't flip a switch during the child's teen years and hope that he or she will welcome a vastly different parenting approach. Parents who do not establish good lines of communication during the preteen years condition their children to communicate in a certain way during their teen years. Parents with a limited interest in their children at one stage of life may find that their children have a limited interest in their parents' involvement at a later stage of life.

There are no easy shortcuts to building and maintaining a strong

---

Father's Business, 1994) gives great prayer helps and specific Scriptures for you to pray over your children. Kimberly Wagner also gives a number of Scriptures that parents can pray for their children's future spouses in her helpful article "Praying for Your Child's Future Mate," *True Woman* (blog), June 9, 2011, https://www.reviveourhearts.com/true-woman/blog/praying-for-your-childs-future-mate/.

relationship with your child. It takes work and time. Relational investments throughout a child's grade school and early teen years typically pay off during the young adult years. They help to lay a strong relational foundation that builds trust and earns a parent the right to be heard. Establishing a strong relationship with your child will likely pay big dividends when that child begins dating. The time you spend with your child today, the way you communicate, and the things you talk about establish relational norms with your child that will either bear fruit in the future or reveal a relational deficiency.

I want to encourage you to banish any thoughts of *influence entitlement*—the assumption that years of sacrifice and service on behalf of your children earn you automatic influence in their lives when they are young adults. Don't expect your child to be open to your input whatever the state of your relationship is, and don't think that your child owes you the opportunity to speak into his or her life simply because you are his or her parent. Young adult children do not have to act on our wisdom. We cannot force them to communicate with us or to live obediently before God.

Influence entitlement is dangerous when a parent hopes to reap a harvest that was never sown relationally with a child. You will influence your child toward a godly marriage and a Jesus-loving spouse not only because you are his or her parent but because you have built a strong relationship with your child so that he or she values your input and involvement.

Be Prepared to Talk about Dating

Plenty of parents are caught off guard when their tween or early teenaged children bring up the topic of dating for the first time. Of course, most of the time, it's not called *dating*. How would you respond if one of these scenarios played itself out in your home?

- Your eleven-year-old daughter would like to go to a movie alone with a boy from school. She insists it's not a date, just two friends spending time together.
- Your daughter's middle school is having a dance, and the

school encourages students to find a date. Your daughter is approached by one of her classmates.

- Valentine's Day is tomorrow, and your thirteen-year-old son wants to get flowers for a female classmate.
- Three of your son's friends are getting together at the mall, and he wants to go. Two of the friends are girls, and one is a guy. You've noticed that one of the girls has been texting your son a lot lately.

How would you respond to these requests? Too many parents think, "What's the harm?" or "It's just puppy love." But nothing good comes from awakening love before it can be acted on in marriage. Your children may not like it, but if they understand that the purpose of dating is to pursue marriage, then they can understand that they aren't ready to date until they are ready for marriage.

Research on adolescent sexual behavior has found that early dating increases the likelihood of premarital sex. In fact, the earlier a young person begins dating, the higher the likelihood that he or she will engage in sex outside marriage. This makes sense. Dating encourages an emotional connection between two individuals, which prompts physical contact such as holding hands or kissing. Physical contact fuels sexual urges. Combine this with immaturity or curiosity, and it is a recipe for disaster. By that point, all that young people need is an opportunity to be alone together.

Nothing good comes from awakening love before the right time. The author of Ecclesiastes tells us that there is a time for everything, and that includes dating (see Eccl. 3:1–8). Dating before a young person is ready to seriously consider marriage is premature.

You need to have a ready response, with solid reasoning, to help grade schoolers and early teens understand why it is best to be patient and wait. Encourage your children to view the early teen years as the season of personal preparation for marriage, not as the time to begin looking for prospects. If they are invited to a dance, asked to go to a movie, or sent a text message by an interested party, they will have the convictions and resolve to kindly say no.

Better yet, don't wait for your child to bring up the topic. Initiate a discussion with your child. The summer after a child's third-grade year is ideal, as this is generally when young people start to think about dating. If your child is older, that's fine. Wait for a teachable moment or initiate a discussion in the near future.

After Your Child Begins Dating

What is the role of a parent when a high school–aged child begins dating? Most parents know that they should be involved, but to what degree and in what ways? Here are four suggestions.

Evaluate

Parents are responsible to determine when a teenage child is ready to date. It is your job to assess your child's maturity level. Responsibility and trustworthiness in one area of life will most likely translate into responsibility and trustworthiness in dating. It is your job not to slam the dating door shut but to raise a responsible, respectful, and mature child who is able to date in a God-honoring way.

You have the freedom to tell your teenage child that he or she is not ready to date. A responsible parent would never hand his or her child the keys to a car until the child was mature enough to handle the weighty responsibility of driving. The same logic applies to dating. Just because your child wants to date doesn't mean you have to say yes. Just because every other young person your child knows has a boyfriend or girlfriend doesn't mean that your child needs one as well.

The reverse is also true. Parents, you have the freedom to tell your child yes. Don't say no for the sake of saying no; this can lead to an exasperated child. If your child is ready to pursue marriage and mature enough to handle this responsibility, then there is no biblical reason why he or she should not date. If you have been preparing for this day, you can use this opportunity as a life milestone to bless your child and speak to the godly man or woman that he or she is becoming.

Who decides when a young person is ready to date? Parents have the final say. Who is better equipped to determine whether a young person is ready to date? I'd say it is individuals who have been married for a couple of decades and do not have their minds clouded by raging hormones! If you have a strong relationship with your child, your no will not feel heavy-handed. Even if he or she does not like your decision, your child will understand that you have made it with his or her long-term interest in mind.

You should also be zealous to help your teenage child discern whether someone is marriage material. How you do this is key. Thoughtful comments, clarifying questions, and listening ears are all good methods to use. After all, who is the better judge of character and compatibility for marriage: someone who has been married for many years and gone through the dating process, or someone who has never before dated or been married? Parents who have established good relationships with their children will have opportunities to be sounding boards and to lovingly speak into critical life decisions.

Communicate

Details about a child's dates and purity are not private information that parents have no business knowing. Discussing dating experiences with your child should be just as comfortable and common as talking about the weather or sports. This will be most attainable if you establish a solid relationship with your teenage child and create a culture in the home in which it is normal to talk about feelings and not keep secrets. If a pattern of secrecy develops, consider this a problem and work to establish better communication.

Your goal is to get past the twenty-question approach to gaining information. You're familiar with what this is like, right? It feels like an interrogation. Information has to be pried out of the child because he or she will not willingly share experiences. Questions such as "Who are you with?" or "Where are you going?" stop at surface-level details (you should still ask these questions but should not stop there). We want to get beyond this, to matters of the heart, and focus on questions such as "What attracts you to this person?" or "Why do you think this person would make a good husband or wife?" We want our children to have regular, open, and honest conversations with us about their dating desires and experiences.

Advise

During the teenage years, many parents and grandparents pull back and become less involved in their children's lives. The dating years are a time when young people need parents to remain engaged. Of course, teenagers won't admit this. (Sometimes they say the exact opposite!) The reality is that your teenage child wants your affection and attention. Your child needs your guidance and affirmation. Culture may tell you that your teenage child needs his or her independence and that separation is a good thing. But this separation becomes unhealthy when it manifests itself in emotional distance, physical isolation, and an overall lack of parental guidance. The teenage years are not the time to pull back. They are a time to get involved.

During the dating days, you should meet and get to know your child's date. Why? According to Proverbs, "There is safety in having many advisors" (Prov. 11:14) and "Without counsel plans fail, but with many advisers they succeed" (Prov. 15:22). Having advisors is good. It leads to wise choices. It helps a person to avoid danger and failure. When it comes to dating, we want to help our young-adult children navigate around many different land mines. In order to do this, we have to be involved and informed. We can't speak into our children's lives if we have stepped out of their world.

You are an advisor to your dating child. In fact, you are your child's *most important* advisor. No human being knows your child better or loves your child more than you do. God has given you, as the parent, the role of shepherding your child, and the dating days are a critical time when your involvement is needed. Step into this role. Take it seriously.

Your parental advice is needed. Your teenage child has an underdeveloped discernment muscle. He or she will have blind spots and is still learning how to make wise decisions. In addition, self-control typically isn't a strength for most teenagers. A heightened sex drive and surging hormones do not help young people make great choices. Given this reality, along with the magnitude of the decisions they are making and the lifelong consequences that will follow, you have every reason to stay involved.

Protect

You also have a role to protect your teenage children. Your involvement, in the form of parental accountability, will help teenagers to protect their purity. Teenagers can never have too much accountability! They need clearly enforced boundaries, alongside the reminder that you love them and want what is best for them. Plenty of young people, even those with the best of intentions and strong convictions, give in to temptation and cross boundaries that they later regret. Your presence will help your children to set and maintain boundaries so that their dating days and future marriages are not filled with regret.

To protect your child, help him or her to avoid compromising situations and discern a date's marital compatibility. Help your child choose the right person and avoid the wrong places. For example, as we saw Matt Chandler point out earlier, few good things happen between 11 p.m. and 1 a.m. on the couch while you are watching a movie alone with a boyfriend or girlfriend. Help your child avoid these kinds of compromising situations.

Parents of daughters have a greater responsibility in this area. I love what Dennis Rainey says to fathers regarding this subject.

> For most girls your daughter's age, the dating years will lead to heartbreak and confusion, if not utter devastation. Peer pressure and the self-focused nature of needing boyfriends will lead many girls to lose all sense of perspective and make some of the worst decisions of their young lives. That's because most girls will be left to fend for themselves by fathers who are too busy, too uneasy, or too afraid to get involved—too quick to assume that everything will be all right. He may know more about the quarterback of his

favorite football team than he does about the young man who's driving away with his daughter tonight.[2]

Father, your daughter needs you. You have a God-given role as protector over her. Don't leave your daughter to fend for herself. Instead, help her to send off and fend off the wrong guys and to protect her purity and select a spouse biblically.

This applies to sons as well. If you want to make sure that your son or daughter's dating days are a success, then have parental influence during this time. It is one of the most important investments you can ever make in your child.

Think back to your own dating days. How would you feel if your teenage child replicated your dating experience? Most parents don't get too excited about this prospect. Most would do things differently if they had a do-over. You can't change your past, but you can protect your child's future.

During Your Child's Dating Years

Involvement with dating teenagers is not about control. It shouldn't result from fear. It has nothing to do with lack of trust. It's about a child's long-term good. It's about sparing children from their selfish passion and sinful tendencies. It's about helping them to arrive at their wedding day sexually pure. It's about helping them to choose a good and godly spouse.

I recently had lunch with a wise father and mother named John and Lorinda—well-respected parents of ten children. The subject of

2. Dennis Rainey, *Interviewing Your Daughter's Date: 30 Minutes Man-To-Man* (Canton, GA: Family Life Publishing, 2012), 4. If you have a daughter, I highly recommend that you read this book. It will give you a newfound appreciation for your role as protector and a strong sense of urgency to actively meet and get to know your daughter's potential dates. Dads, the fact that someone wants to date your daughter means that he wants your job as her sacrificial leader. Dennis Rainey provides a very practical and extremely helpful road map on how to make sure that he is fit for the task.

a parent's role in dating was on my mind, so I asked them to share how they navigate dating with their children. They said something that all parents need to hear: *there is no perfect formula.*

The way you prepare your child for a godly marriage is flexible, to some degree. It may look different from one child to the next and from family to family. God has not explicitly dictated many things related to the pre-marriage process in Scripture. He has given us principles and has entrusted the rest to us. This Christian freedom is welcome to some but is challenging for those who want a detailed checklist to follow.

We want the formula, right? We want seven steps to a child's perfect marriage. No such formula exists. The closest thing to a formula is this: seek first the kingdom of God (see Matt. 6:33), and "whatever you eat or drink or whatever you do, do it all for the glory of God" (1 Cor. 10:31). All that your child does, including dating, should be pleasing to God. If your child seeks Christ and lives to glorify God, you will probably be pleased with their dating results. If your child internalizes biblical convictions about marriage and holiness, you should like the outcome.

This isn't an excuse to be an absent parent. It doesn't mean that you should close this book and stop intentionally helping your child to prepare for marriage. Instead, it releases you from legalism. It allows you to be gracious to other Christ-loving families who choose to help their children pursue marriage a little differently from how you choose to do it. It frees you to adjust your methods to each child and each situation.

This is not to suggest that the truths of Scripture are elastic. In the next chapter, we'll talk about who God has clearly forbidden us to date or marry. We have already talked about sexual ethics and the absolute purity that God expects outside the bounds of marriage. However, there is freedom regarding what age your child begins to date, what time your child is required home at night, and what rules you set in place to help your child protect his or her sexual purity.

Shower your child with prayer, work closely with your child

to evaluate his or her readiness for dating, and be actively involved as an advisor while your child dates. There is flexibility in how you do that.

Courageous Conversations

1. How do you feel about the state of your relationship with your mom and dad? Are you satisfied with it, or are there areas that you would like to see improved?
2. What should be a parent's role in a teenager's date life?
3. Parent, what role would you like to have in your child's date life? Why?
4. Young person, what role would you like your parent to have? Why?
5. Read Proverbs 11:14 and 15:22. What important role does this suggest that a parent has? How would this apply to dating?
6. Read Ephesians 6:1–2. How does this passage apply to young people who are interested in dating?
7. In light of Ephesians 6:1–2, if parents create dating limitations, how should a teenage child respond?
8. Who gets to determine when a young person is ready to date?
9. What are your expectations for communication between you and your parents leading up to dating and when you are dating?
10. As you begin dating, how can your parent pray for you?
11. Read 1 Corinthians 10:31. How would taking this passage seriously affect your dating days?

WHOM SHOULD
YOUR CHILD DATE?

Following Biblical Guidelines

Wouldn't it be great if a chorus of angels sang when we first laid eyes on our future spouse? Even better would be the audible voice of God saying something along the lines of, "This is your future spouse, with whom I am well pleased." My guess is that the heavens will not part and the angels will not sing for your child when he or she is trying to decide whom to date and marry. God is a big God who is capable of those things, so this could possibly happen, but I suggest that you have a backup plan ready. You know, just in case.

How will you help your child discern the will of God in marriage? When it comes to choosing whom to date and marry, plenty of Christians are frozen with fear, filled with indecision, and prone to second guesses. This is a big decision. We don't want to get it wrong. So, as parents, how do we get it right as we help our children understand the will of God for marriage?

Seeking God's Guidance: What Not to Do

First, don't encourage your child to pursue a message from God apart from the Bible. The misleading idea is that all the person needs to do is to ask and listen. If he or she listens hard enough and long enough, Jesus will answer as a quiet voice in one's mind or by providing a strong feeling accompanied by a sense of peace. We know that God communicates with us, the logic goes, so why wouldn't Jesus personally communicate with us in our minds?

A second wrong approach is to seek a mystical experience. Here are two hypothetical examples. Using this method, your daughter prays to God for guidance on whether to continue or to break off a dating relationship. Soon after praying, she spots a billboard for an online dating service as she drives down the road. She wonders if this is God's way of telling her to break up and date someone else. Or, while trying to decide whether to date someone, your son goes outside for some fresh air, only to spot a cloud shaped like a heart. Is the heart a sign that God wants your son to start dating this girl? The sign could be anything—a song, a conversation, a symbol, even a piece of toast with a person's face on it.

At the surface, these approaches sound spiritual and appear pious. The problem is that they aren't biblical. They are nothing more than subjective guesses that operate as substitutes for the authoritative Word of God. These methods lack spiritual discernment and set a dangerous precedent because they raise questions about the authority and legitimacy of the message. How does a person verify that words or signs are truly from God? How does a person differentiate between a passing thought and the work of the Holy Spirit? Is a personal message from God to be treated in the same way that the rest of God's words are treated in Scripture—as inspired words with the full authority of God? If yes, then we have new words to add to the canon of Scripture. If no, how are we to understand these messages, and how do they relate to the rest of the Bible? Are messages from God the normative experience for all Christians or just a random experience for one Christian?

Mystical experiences and extrabiblical messages from God operate as substitute sources for the Bible in the decision-making process. Rather than looking to the wisdom that God has already provided in Scripture, an individual following these approaches looks to non-authoritative, unverifiable, and subjective external sources. That is problematic. Theologically, it reveals a lack of belief in the sufficiency of Scripture. Such behavior states that the Bible is not enough, that it doesn't address the topic, and that a supplemental source is needed in order to make a sound decision.

Seeking God's Guidance: What to Do

The Bible claims to offer everything that the Christian needs in order to make decisions and live a godly life (see 2 Peter 1:3). This includes dating. Our children don't need to lay out a fleece before God when they seek guidance from him, because God provides answers in the Bible and gives young people big-picture criteria to keep in mind as they pursue a future spouse. The problem is that some people want more than that—a seven-step guide to dating and an individual confirmation from God for their choice of spouse.

God doesn't need to work like that. His confirmation appears in the Bible in the form of his commands and guidelines. For example, Christians are told not to marry non-Christians. This may sound unspiritual, but your daughter doesn't need to ask God whether she should date the nice non-Christian guy who just asked her out. Sure, he's handsome. And funny. He serves at the local food shelter and loves little kids. He comes from a good family. He even goes to church. But God has already given his answer in the Bible. Christians are not to marry—and therefore should not date—non-Christians. Your daughter's job is to apply God's wisdom to dating.

What about when guidance on dating isn't black and white in Scripture? Thankfully, God provides general principles for marriage and relationships. Your job is to apply them to dating and to teach them to your children. We want our children to use the Bible as the filter to decide who is datable and who isn't. If the person your child would like to pursue meets the biblical guidelines, then God says yes to this person. If the guidelines aren't being met, then pause and look elsewhere.

Your child can use four steps to decide whom he or she should date.[1]

Search the Bible

While the word *dating* is not in the Bible, God has plenty to say about the type of companions a person should pursue and also avoid. As we'll see later in this chapter, God is clear that a Christian should not marry a non-Christian or someone divorced for unbiblical reasons.

Seek Godly Counsel

The Bible speaks highly of individuals who have multiple advisors, seek second opinions, and invite others to speak into their lives in order to sharpen them. Ask your child, "Do your family and friends think it is wise for you to date and marry the individual you are interested in?" Young people do well to pay attention to the wisdom of others—especially their parents and grandparents.

Pray

Ask God for clarity and peace. My parents taught me that if my spirit is not at peace about a decision, I should pay attention. Uneasiness may be the Holy Spirit's work. My dad had a saying that has served me well: "When in doubt, don't do." I'm a strategic person, and I'm willing to take calculated risks, so this has been a helpful guideline in life. It has helped me to slow down, pay attention to red flags, and avoid poor choices.

Act

If a decision aligns with God's laws and wisdom, if parents and godly friends approve, and if God's Spirit has given you peace, then the last step is to act. Your child can move forward with confidence and freedom. Ask the girl out, or let the wedding bells ring. Because

1. Adapted from Kevin DeYoung's book *Just Do Something: A Liberating Approach to Finding God's Will* (Chicago: Moody, 2014), 103–4.

that is the goal, right? When the right one comes along, step out in faith.

Biblical Guidelines for Choosing a Date

How does your child know whom to date? The Bible has plenty to say about marriage that informs the dating process. The Bible also offers general principles that every believer can use to navigate the mundane, routine, everyday decisions that he or she makes. It calls this *wisdom*. Wisdom is God's truth applied to life. It's moral skill-fulness. It's the ability to take God's principles for relationships and marriage and apply them to dating. God doesn't provide a step-by-step dating guide. Instead, he gives the Christian general guidelines and the freedom to make decisions within the boundaries he has set.

Let's look at those boundaries and guidelines now.

Date Only Committed Christians

Is it ever okay for a Christian to date a non-Christian? Try asking your child this question. You might be surprised by the answer.

Here are common responses that I have received over fifteen years of asking students this question:

- Yes, as long as it's not a serious relationship.
- Yes, as long as we don't get married.
- It's okay if the goal is to help the other person become a Christian.[2]

These are dangerous answers that lead to future problems if the dating relationship results in marriage. A destructive line of romantic thinking holds that if you find the one you are really interested in, who makes your heart go pitter-patter, then it doesn't matter what this person believes, whether he or she is a Christian, and if he or she loves Jesus or lives obediently to God.

2. This is known as missionary dating.

223

What matters most, according to this belief, is the chemistry between two individuals. Many young people fool themselves into thinking that they will work the Jesus thing out later and that love will overcome religious beliefs. This is faulty thinking. Faith needs to be the strength of a relationship, not the cause for division. If the purpose of dating is to find a spouse, then young people should date only the people they would potentially marry.

Levels of Relationships

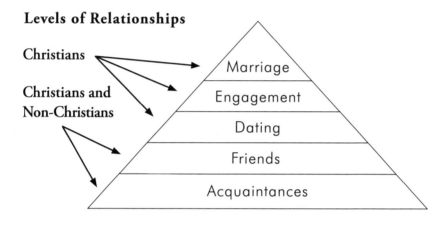

The Bible is clear that a Christian is to marry only another Christian. Second Corinthians 6:14–15 states, "Do not be yoked together with unbelievers. For what do righteousness and wickedness have in common? Or what fellowship can light have with darkness? . . . What does a believer have in common with an unbeliever?" (NIV). Our children should yoke themselves to those who will be pulling in the same direction that they themselves are headed in life. Otherwise, the marriage becomes a tug of war and the home becomes a battlefield. It is not good for two individuals with different beliefs or perspectives on life to marry each other. Richard and Sharon Phillips write,

> A Christian has no business dating someone who has not come to faith in Christ. A relationship between a Christian and an unbeliever is powerless to enjoy the blessings of Christ's redeeming work, for the simple reason that it is based on unbelief and

rebellion rather than faith in God's Word. . . . This, like all of God's
. . . commands, is not a cruel barrier to our happiness, but a loving
restriction that preserves us for God's blessing.[3]

Our children will base their marriages on one of two founda-
tions: rebellion to Christ or the redemption of Christ. One unites;
the other divides. One invites blessing; the other invites curses.
A marriage relationship between a believer and an unbeliever is established in direct disobedience to 2 Corinthians 6:14–15. Under no
circumstance should your child ever date a non-Christian. This is an
unbending requirement of Scripture and the single most important
thing to consider when looking for a future spouse.

Remind your child that many people call themselves Christians
but live nothing like Christ demands. Claiming the name of Christ
is one thing; living like Christ is another. True faith in Jesus leads to
life-altering beliefs and behaviors, which should be recognizable in
the fruit of godly character.

Remember the Roles of a Husband and a Wife

If God's role for a husband is to be the spiritual leader, sacrificial
servant, protector, and provider in marriage, then daughters should
use these important criteria to discern whom to date. If God's role
for a wife is to be a willing follower who builds her home and raises
a family, then sons should use these valuable criteria to decide whom
to pursue for marriage.

In this way, we take God's principles for marriage and back-
track them into the dating relationship. Young men look for a
future wife who will make a great helpmate, and young women
look for a future husband who will embrace sacrificial leadership as
the marriage head. Young women should pay attention to whether
a young man has a servant's heart, a good work ethic, and a loving

3. Richard D. Phillips and Sharon L. Phillips, *Holding Hands, Holding Hearts:
Recovering a Biblical View of Christian Dating* (Phillipsburg, NJ: P&R Publishing,
2006), 55.

demeanor, and whether he displays spiritual leadership in other contexts. Young men should pay attention to a young woman's attitudes, her willingness to follow, how she respects others, and the importance she places on the home.

How can you help your child do this?

Model what you want your child to choose. In your marriage, point out what sacrificial leadership and willing followership looks like, and tell your child that this is what he or she is looking for in a future spouse. Provide concrete examples so that your child can recognize it when he or she sees it in others.

Encourage your child to be with a date in different contexts. The goal is to discover who the person truly is. Different contexts reveal a person's true character. Surprise is never a good thing in marriage. Our children should be around their potential spouses long enough to see their hearts. If the speed of the relationship outpaces your child's knowledge of the other person's character, then it needs to slow down.

Encourage your child to define a dating relationship. Before dating someone, your child should know the other person's intentions. Taking it day by day or leaving a relationship undefined is a recipe for a broken heart. Your child should not enter into a dating relationship unless both parties are equally committed and have the overall goal of marriage. When one person is more committed to a relationship than the other, painful disappointment usually results.

Avoid Certain Kinds of People

The Bible, especially in the book of Proverbs, spends quite a bit of time telling young people whom to avoid. Parents are wise to apply this instruction to the dating process. Here are three examples.

Disobedient individuals. Proverbs 1 warns young people not to associate with individuals who plot evil, because in the end your child will be caught in a trap if he or she does this (see Prov. 1:10–19).

Much heartache comes from pursuing a spouse who refuses to walk obediently before the Lord (see Prov. 3:33). Psalm 1:1 reminds young people, "Blessed is the man who walks not in the counsel of the wicked." The word *blessed* means "O, how very happy." Happy is the young person who does not date or marry an ungodly person.

Young people can ask two questions about a potential date:

- Is there a pattern of unbroken, habitual sin in this person's life, in place of a repentant heart?
- Does the person know what the Lord requires but refuse to obey?

If the answer to either question is yes, then this person should not be pursued.

Pleasure-seeking individuals. Teach your child to avoid individuals who believe it is not wrong to pursue sexual pleasure outside marriage (see Prov. 30:20). Proverbs teaches that it is a blessing to be spared from this person (see Prov. 2:16; 6:24). The individual who makes sexual compromises outside marriage has set the precedent for making sexual compromises while married. Such behavior reveals the character trait of unfaithfulness, and an unfaithful person is not desirable for lifelong marriage. Encourage your child to ask, is my potential date more interested in personal pleasure or in purity of heart?

Quarrelsome individuals. Proverbs says that it is better to live in the corner of an attic than to be around a nagging person (see Prov. 21:9; 25:24). It also says that it is better to be in the desert than to be around a quarrelsome woman (see Prov. 21:19). The Bible tells young people to avoid being around those who are argumentative, angry, and gossipy. Words are not worthless. They are windows into a person's heart. They reveal who a person really is on the inside. Ugly words reveal an ugly heart. Therefore, train your child to pay close attention to the words of others and to avoid dating someone whose words are not controlled. Is a potential date generally argumentative, or agreeable? Is he or she angry, or patient? Does he or she speak poorly, or highly, of others? If this feels petty, remember that communication problems top the list of issues that many couples experience in marriage.

If you are looking for a great study to do with your child, read through Proverbs specifically in order to identify whom the book encourages young people to avoid. It is valuable to make a "do not date" list of character traits to avoid in a potential spouse. This worthwhile activity will create a shared foundation that you can refer back to as you help your child to evaluate dates for marriage.

Identify Who Is to Be Desired as a Spouse

Did you ever make a list of what you were looking for in a spouse? Most people do. Humor is almost always at the top. Physical attractiveness is also popular. Godliness is usually on there. How about athleticism? Intelligence? And on and on the list goes. If you like lists, great. There is nothing wrong with making a list of desirable items for a future spouse. If your child makes a list, help him or her to differentiate between preferences and nonnegotiable items.

The only way to do this is to search the Scriptures in order to know what God requires in a spouse. That list is relatively short. Again, Proverbs is helpful for this task. According to Proverbs, the following individuals are to be desired as a spouse:

An upright individual (Prov. 3:32). This individual does what is right without compulsion, without reward, and when no one is watching. Upright men and women have integrity. They want to please God. They choose the path of righteousness instead of the path of wickedness. In Proverbs, they are known as wise individuals who apply God's truth to life (see Prov. 9:9). Proverbs reminds young people that they will be blessed if they keep God's ways and walk in his path (see Prov. 8:32). Likewise, they will be blessed if they find a spouse who keeps God's ways. Such a person has found favor from the Lord (see Prov. 8:35).

An individual who honors his or her parents (Prov. 10:1). How young people respond to their parents is a good indication of how they will respond to a future spouse. How they live out their roles with their parents provides a clue as to how they will operate in their roles as future husbands or wives. Children are commanded to honor their parents. Does your child's potential date do this? If he or she regularly dishonors his or her parents and brings sadness to them, why would this behavior change in marriage?

A hardworking individual (Prov. 6:6). Scripture never speaks highly of idleness. The sluggard who loves to sleep can anticipate financial challenges in the future (see Prov. 10:4–5). A hardworking person is desirable as a spouse (see Prov. 31:27–28). What is a potential date's work ethic? What are his or her aspirations and ambitions? If his or her work ethic is poor and ambitions are few, that is a good indication that the person will not be a good provider, especially if he is male. Does he or she desire education? Is he or she a willing learner?

A faithful individual (Prov. 5:15–18). One of the heart issues that fuel unfaithfulness is greed. People who have not learned to be content with what they have, including with their spouses, invite problems. The Bible commands spouses to rejoice in each other. Help your child to seek a loyal companion by taking seriously any signs of unfaithfulness during the dating days.

Know What Qualities Are Less Important

The Bible does not single out as important many attributes that people commonly desire in a spouse, such as humor, physical attractiveness, and athletic ability. When looking for a spouse, young people should keep in mind that "charm is deceptive, and beauty is fleeting; but a woman who fears the LORD is to be praised" (Prov. 31:30). Charisma should never be more important than godly character or physical beauty more desired than inner beauty.

American culture tells young people that physical attractiveness and earning potential are the most important things to look for in a spouse, and that character follows these. This is backward. Physical attractiveness is not unimportant. But it is not the primary foundation for a relationship. Pursuing a person whose outward appearance is attractive is a losing strategy. (If you have a son, this is critical for you to help him understand.) Young people must look past bodies and get to know their dates' hearts. Why? At some point, appearances change. Hair goes gray. Wrinkles appear. Weight is gained. If physical attraction is holding the relationship together, then what happens when it disappears? The reality is, godliness is attractive to godly people. We want to help our children be attracted to Christlike character more than all else.

Take Red Flags Seriously

Many young people ignore warning signs, to their own detriment. Your child will think highly of the person he or she is dating, but he or she has to think objectively. Warning signs should not be discounted as insignificant. Red flags to take seriously include addiction, abuse, deception, workaholism, unfaithfulness, and narcissistic tendencies.

Marrying someone with the hope or expectation of significant transformation is never wise. In fact, it is false optimism that often leads to major disappointment. If your child is not satisfied with the person he or she is dating, then your child should not marry that person.

Whatever your child experiences while dating, he or she can expect while married. People who have outbursts of anger and treat their dates harshly will continue to do so in marriage. Dates who are untrustworthy before marriage will likely be untrustworthy in marriage. Dates who are lazy or irresponsible before marriage will likely be lazy and irresponsible in marriage.

Seems like common sense, right? The problem is that we tend to give people the benefit of the doubt when we are fond of them. We think that they just had a bad day. We chalk up their behavior to stress or tiredness. Problems arise when *we assume that a person will change when married.* Assumptions of change are dangerous. Some people change and make great spouses. But plenty do not. Many young people end up in bad marriages because they marry on potential. Train your child to take character flaws and red flags seriously.

Choose Your Dates Carefully

Many parents, in an effort not to cause waves, step on toes, or cause tension in a relationship, affirm whomever their child is attracted to. This is a mistake and is one area in which parents need to exert as much influence as possible.

Eventually, one of your child's dates will be his or her mate. This should lead to a selective dating process. If a person isn't marriageable, then he or she isn't datable. Plenty of young people begin casually dating people whom they don't intend to marry, only to find their hearts growing fond of them over time. Then they are faced with a difficult dilemma—at least in their own minds. Should they end the relationship and experience heartache, or continue the relationship and marry an ungodly spouse?

Proactively talk through criteria for selecting a spouse *before* the dating days begin so that you have points of reference with your child as he or she enters into the dating period. My parents did this masterfully with me, regarding both my selection of friends and my selection of dates. In one instance, we were talking about a potential date. My parents never voiced disapproval, but apparently they felt apprehension. They asked a single question about what I thought the young woman's choice of clothing revealed about her heart. It was never a discussion, just a rhetorical question to get me thinking. It worked, and I never pursued her. My parents had skillfully pointed out immodesty without a direct assault on the person or my choices. They had the foresight to talk about inner beauty and outward appearance before I began dating, so this reference reaped what was already sown. And they had my heart. Had my parents not had my heart, it is unlikely that I would have been willing to listen and follow.

Dating that doesn't take the spiritual condition of the other person into consideration will cause considerable heartache. Individual devotion to the Lord is the foundation for a strong and lasting marriage. It should also be the foundation for whomever a young person dates.

A dating relationship, like a marriage, should point to Christ and honor him. Others should look at your child's dating relationship and think more highly of Jesus Christ. A dating relationship that honors Jesus is one that seeks to help the other person become more like Christ.

This is precisely what husbands are told to do in Ephesians 5:26–27. They are given the task of helping their wives to grow in sanctification as they are washed with the Word of God, so that they will be holy before the Lord. Husbands are given the role as the spiritual leader in marriage, and young men should understand that this is one of their primary roles in the dating process. As the spiritual leader, a young man should want to see his date grow in her relationship with Jesus. This is to be a desired outcome of dating, just as it is a desired outcome of marriage. Ask your child, "Did you become more like Jesus as a result of this date?" and "If others observed your date, do they think more highly of Christ as a result?"

Knowing When to Say Yes

Your child doesn't need to base dating decisions on subjective feelings or mystical experiences. The heavens don't need to part and a chorus of angels don't need to sing when our children first lay eyes on their future spouses. The Bible provides the criteria that our children need in order to discern who to date and eventually marry. I'll summarize them with three Cs:

- Marry a *Christian*
- who has godly *character*
- and is *committed* to the covenant of marriage.

God doesn't have ten boxes for your child to check before getting married. He has one primary criterion: marry a Christian. Wise people consider his other guidelines in the decision-making process. They avoid marrying individuals with ungodly character and pursue those who imitate Christ and are committed to marriage for life (i.e., are not divorced for unbiblical reasons). If your child finds such a person, the two like each other, and you aren't alarmed by anything, then they should probably get married.

Assuming that a couple plans to marry, they should be married sooner rather than later. Delaying marriage only invites sexual temptation. Biblical references to "the wife of your youth" suggest that marrying young isn't unprecedented and isn't out of the question. I don't mean that teenagers should start getting married. But couples don't need to date for years and years. Once two people have decided to get married, they should get married. And parents shouldn't stand in the way. Don't assume that your child has to have a four-year degree, no debt, or a job before getting married. If God doesn't require it, you shouldn't either. And if you do, you're an accidental Pharisee. You've created rules where God has said there is freedom. Instead, know that your child wants you to affirm his or her future spouse and bless the marriage.

Kevin DeYoung writes,

> I know this will sound very unromantic (especially to some of the ladies), but don't think that there is only one person on the whole planet to whom you could be happily married. You're not looking for that one puzzle piece that will interlock with yours. "You complete me" may sound magically romantic, but it's not true. . . .
>
> Don't think that *I've met this great gal, but what if she's not the one? What if the one is in Boise and I haven't found her yet?* . . . The problem with the myth of "the one" is that it assumes that affection is the glue that holds the marriage together, when really it is your commitment to marriage that safeguards the affection. So ditch the myth and get hitched.[4]

---

4. DeYoung, *Just Do Something*, 107. This book includes an excellent chapter on how to discern God's will in marriage. If you have a young adult child who is

If God's criteria are met, your child is free to date and marry whomever he or she wishes. God's guidelines are meant to be freeing. They clearly reveal who is in bounds and who is out of bounds for marriage. The young person who obeys the Lord and seeks a future mate according to God's standards will experience what Proverbs 18:22 describes: "He who finds a good wife [or husband] finds a good thing and obtains favor from the LORD." Happy dating!

Courageous Conversations

1. What guidelines should you use in deciding whom to date?
2. How can the biblical role of a husband or wife be useful when you are choosing whom to date and marry?
3. Read Proverbs 18:22. What are two outcomes of choosing a good spouse?
4. Based on the following verses, whom should you avoid dating?
   a. Proverbs 1:10–15
   b. 1 Corinthians 15:33
   c. Proverbs 2:16
   d. Proverbs 9:13
   e. Proverbs 21:9
5. According to Proverbs, what traits are desirable in a future spouse?
   a. Psalm 1:1
   b. Proverbs 31:30
   c. Proverbs 3:32
   d. Proverbs 8:32
   e. Proverbs 10:1
   f. Proverbs 6:6
   g. Proverbs 31:27–28
   h. Proverbs 5:15–18

---

trying to decide whether to marry a certain person, I encourage you to purchase this book.

6. Read 2 Corinthians 6:14–15. What does it mean to be "unequally yoked"? What guideline does this teach about whom you should date and marry?

7. According to 2 Corinthians 6:14–15, is it ever okay for a Christian to date a non-Christian? Why or why not?

8. Read Mark 10:11–12. What guideline does this passage teach about whom you should not marry?

9. Summarize the criteria the Bible provides for whom to date and marry.

10. Homework: Find someone at your church who is married to a non-Christian, and have your child ask the believing spouse, "What's been your experience being married to someone who does not share the same beliefs as you?" Make sure that he or she asks how this has impacted life decisions such as use of money, raising of children, handling of conflict, and commitment to the marriage.

CONCLUSION

FINAL THOUGHTS

Your child's choice of a husband or wife is the second most important decision your child will make in life, after his or her response to Christ. He or she needs your wisdom in order to pursue marriage in God's timing and in God's ways. If your child is not given a biblical, high, Christ-centered view of marriage, he or she will likely live with distorted views and destructive practices. Therefore, you must be intentional to raise a child whose marriage honors God, impacts generations to come with the gospel, and is a witness to the world about the love of the Savior for his people.

We live at a time when many people have a low view of marriage. Our culture has taken that which God created good—marriage and sex—and has twisted it into a means of self-indulgence that focuses on the love of one person for another. Our culture tells young people that they need a boyfriend or girlfriend. It tells them that sexual exploration is a rite of passage. It tells them that it is normal, good, and healthy to indulge in whatever sexual desires they may have.

Your child needs to understand his or her sexuality through the lens of the Bible, not the other way around—to seek satisfaction in Christ alone, to learn sexual self-control, and to understand that sex points to the deeper love of the Savior for his church.

By the time your child is a young adult, you should be putting the finishing touches on years of conversations about sex, purity, and marriage. As I hope I have shown throughout this book, opportunities to talk about these topics present themselves often. You can be confident as you use the Bible to prepare your child from an early age for a gospel-centered marriage.

As you embark upon this journey with your child, may your conversations be rich. May your relationship be intimate. May your teaching be biblical. May your child's holiness be high. Most importantly, may your picture of marriage be Christ-centered.

APPENDIX A

A WORD TO GRANDPARENTS

God designed grandparents to be key partners with parents in raising children to treasure Jesus Christ. I hope that many Christian grandparents use this book to intentionally shepherd young people toward a biblical view of marriage and to encourage them to make God-glorifying life choices. Here are six suggestions to help grandparents successfully prepare grandchildren for marriage.

Understand Your Role

God has given grandparents the role of building a Christ-centered family heritage by passing on faith to future generations. He designed the role of grandparents to center on the evangelism and discipleship of grandchildren. God instructs grandparents to teach grandchildren the Word of the Lord (see Deut. 4:9; 6:2; Ps. 78:5) and to tell grandchildren the work of the Lord in their own life (see Ps. 78:4). Grandparents are given a God-ordained role that is not interchangeable with anyone else and are an essential component in raising future generations to know, love, and serve Christ. If you are interested in learning more about the biblical role of a grandparent, culture's erroneous message to grandparents, and ways to be a disciple-making grandparent, then check out my book *Biblical Grandparenting*.[1]

Discuss Plans with Adult Children

Grandparents should discuss, with adult children, their desire to speak into a grandchild's life on the subject of marriage, dating, sex, or purity before addressing the topics with grandchildren. A conversation on the front end honors parents as the primary influencers of their children's faith, eliminates surprises, communicates expectations, and ensures that parent and grandparent are in agreement about a plan and a path forward. This step helps grandparents and parents work together to disciple a child instead of allowing a well-intentioned grandparent to act without a parent's knowledge or invitation.

Grandparents should communicate three things to adult children.

- Tell your adult child that you have been given an important role by God to disciple your grandchild. You may want to show your adult child Deuteronomy 4:9 and 6:2.
- Tell your adult child that one way you want to invest in your grandchild is to help him or her prepare for marriage. You may want to provide a copy of this book to your adult child in order to help him or her understand the need for this and the approach you wish to take.
- Ask for permission and discuss how your adult child would like you to be involved. You may want to provide concrete ideas, such as studying the Bible with your grandchild on these subject matters or providing a special gift that symbolizes a biblical truth.

---

1. Josh Mulvihill, *Biblical Grandparenting: Exploring God's Design, Culture's Messages and Disciple-Making Methods to Pass Faith to Future Generations* (Chaska, MN: atFamily Press, 2016).

Invest in Your Child's Marriage

You will help your grandchildren to prepare for marriage by helping your adult children to maintain a strong marriage centered on Christ. Here are four ways you can do that.

- Personally invest in the spiritual growth of your adult child.
- Provide Bible-based resources such as books or articles on marriage.
- Offer to pay for your adult child to attend a marriage conference.
- Watch your grandchildren for an evening, a weekend, or even a week so that your adult children can spend time together building their marriage.

If you watch your grandchildren, be sure not to undermine the priorities or practices of your adult child. If grandma and grandpa give grandchildren lots of sugar, let them stay up late, or do not enforce the same guidelines that parents so, then the reentry period when grandchildren return home is difficult, and an adult child may decide that the cost of reestablishing a regular routine is not worth the short-term benefits. Key areas that often cause tension include what the child eats, when the child sleeps, and what the child watches on television. I encourage you to initiate a brief conversation with your adult child in order to determine what he or she desires in these areas.

Model a Godly Marriage

My grandparents, Carl and Allie, were married for over sixty-five years. They modeled faithfulness, forgiveness, and companionship. In an era when divorce is common, this is an incredible gift and a strong legacy. Your goal is to give this same gift to your grandchildren. Grandchildren will learn from what you say, but they will also learn by observing your marriage. Many young people pattern their lives after parents and grandparents—whether good or bad.

Grey divorce, when spouses divorce later in life, has become more common. If you are a grandparent considering divorce, know that it will have a lasting impact on your grandchildren and will affect their view of marriage. When you fight for your marriage, you are fighting for the marriages of future generations because you model how to work through conflict, demonstrate the importance of keeping one's vows, and become a living example of the sanctity of marriage according to Scripture.

Be a Source of Wisdom

You have a lifetime of knowledge and experience on relationships and marriage. Look for opportunities to intentionally share with your family what you have learned. This can take many forms, such as sharing the successes and failures of your own life or speaking into the dating decisions of a grandchild. It may also mean that you operate as a sounding board to an adult child who is navigating the dating and marriage years with their children for the first time. Proverbs states that young people benefit from having many advisors in their life (see Prov. 15:22). You are a key advisor to your children and grandchildren. Words of wisdom will be received if you have developed and maintained an intimate relationship with your family.

Be a Surrogate for Single Parents

Grandparents of single parents can provide the model of what it means to be a godly husband or wife. Ideally, boys learn to be godly husbands from other men and girls learn to be godly wives from other women. If your grandchildren do not have the same-gendered parent actively investing in them to prepare them for marriage, prayerfully consider stepping into this role.

God has designed families so that children have six voices—two parents and four grandparents—speaking into their lives. What a blessing it is for a young person to have multiple voices preparing him or her for marriage. Parenting is a large task, and God created grand*parents* to share in the effort of raising young people to think and live in a way that honors Christ. I encourage you to embrace this role and use this resource to disciple your grandchildren so that they have a biblical view of marriage and pursue marriage in a God-honoring way.

Appendix B

The Wisdom of Faithfulness (Proverbs 5)

For the teacher or parent who reads Proverbs 5 and believes it is inappropriate for a child to hear these things, I must point out a few things: (1) Proverbs was written to children (see Prov. 5:1, 7) making it critical for them to hear this message. (2) Proverbs is inspired by God. He chose the topic, not me. I trust that God knows what a child needs to hear. (3) Society has distorted marriage and encourages children to seek sexual pleasure apart from marriage (and thus they need to learn that the desire for sex is a desire for marriage). Children are bombarded by this message from the media, from school (as early as kindergarten), and from friends. The parent who remains silent on this subject creates a void that is being filled by ungodly voices and is shaping a child's heart. Of course, discretion is needed when you speak on this subject. Children need to be told the truth, but they can be told the truth in a PG way. That is the goal.

For the teacher: There are a few things you must know when teaching this subject matter. First, always err on the side of caution. Be conservative with your words and choose them carefully. When you are dealing with this subject, a useful motto to remember is: when in doubt, keep it out! Second, I believe it is primarily the parents' role to speak of these matters to their children. I want to set the table for parents, but not steal their thunder. Third, do not glorify past sins. If you have sinned in this area, don't share nitty-gritty details, but tell the children that the Bible is telling the truth and that consequences are real. Fourth, be sensitive, as many children are living with the reality of marriages that are struggling or have failed due to unfaithfulness. Fifth, you are teaching the principles of joy and faithfulness in marriage, not an anatomy or health lesson. Don't venture where the Bible does not go. We can say a lot without having to say much.

About this lesson: It was written with fifth and sixth graders in mind. Therefore, if used with elementary children, it should be adjusted and made more conservative. Please make the focus of this lesson the joy of faithfulness and the cost of unfaithfulness.

— Pray with children to begin class —

Introduction

A child is encouraged to listen to a parent's instruction so that the child may learn discretion and choose faithfulness in marriage over temporary moments of physical pleasure. In Proverbs 4:20–27, young people are taught that the body can be an instrument of good or of evil. Thus, young people need to learn to rule their bodies, or their bodies will rule them. In Proverbs 5, the young person is given a real-life situation in which he or she will need to learn self-control. Proverbs 5 talks about the pain of choosing sin and the joys of marriage—a critical message for young people to hear today.

Teaching Points

Read Proverbs 5:1–23 aloud from the Bible (you may want to break this up into chunks)

What should a young person know about faithfulness in marriage? (See object lesson)

1. **Impurity sounds good and looks good, but it leads to bitterness and death** (see vv. 1–6). Sin always looks appealing, but it only momentarily delivers its promises. Proverbs does not sugarcoat the truth; it wants children to know the consequences of future decisions. The person who has chosen to enter into a physical relationship with someone who is not his or her husband or wife is said to be on the path to hell (see v. 5). And those who seek this person's company may follow, because they are in danger of being influenced to do evil.

2. **There is a cost to unfaithfulness in marriage** (see vv. 7–14). God never allows us to sin successfully. Proverbs exhorts young people to flee from sin and stay as far away from it as possible (see v. 8). The chapter reveals four costs of unfaithfulness:
   - **Honor** (v. 9). Sexual sin brings about the loss of respect in the eyes of others due to a stained character. Sexual sin puts a black mark on the sinner's reputation. Lack of integrity always leads to a loss in credibility.
   - **Time** (vv. 9–10). Time that could have been used to build a relationship was used to destroy it. People who sin sexually use time to inflict wounds on themselves and on those they love.
   - **Wealth** (v. 10). The unfaithful give their resources to others.
   - **Regret** (vv. 11–13). The unfaithful must live their whole lives knowing that they made a foolish choice. In the end, it brings a person to utter ruin both in this life and in eternity (see v. 14).

3. **Happiness in marriage is the outcome of two things** (see vv. 15–19). God tells young people how to have a blessed, or happy, marriage (see v. 18):
   - **Rejoice in your future spouse** (v. 18). Couples often criticize, complain about, and wish for changes in each other. Rather than complain about the negative traits or habits

that a spouse may have, a young person is to purposefully rejoice in all the positive things that his or her spouse brings to the marriage. God commands young people to rejoice in their spouses. They are to choose joy. They are to celebrate the good things.

- **Enjoy love** (v. 19). Spouses are to enjoy each other physically, and this helps them to maintain marital faithfulness. "At all times" and "intoxicated" suggest there is a regularity and consistency to the physical elements of marriage. Your future wife or husband is for you alone (see vv. 15–17). God's plan is one man and one woman for one lifetime. When that path is deviated from, one can expect major problems.

4. **God is watching and sees all of your actions** (see v. 21). Nothing is hidden from the Lord. No deed goes unnoticed. Purity and intimacy must be protected.

5. **Physical urges are to be controlled** (see v. 23). In Proverbs 5, the father challenges his son to discipline his sexual urges. The exact words of the father are "He dies for lack of discipline" (v. 23). One of the most important things to learn is self-control (see Titus 2:5–6). The Bible teaches young people to run from, rather than embrace, sexual urges that do not align with God's standards.

Object Lesson

If you are married, invite your spouse to be your object lesson. Have your spouse stand next to you, and ask the children, "Would it be right for me to kiss another man/woman like I kiss my husband/ wife?" Also ask, "Would it be right for me to hug another man/ woman like I hug my husband/wife?" The Bible teaches that if I do, there will be costs of my unfaithfulness (and then teach point number two above). The Bible also teaches that if I am faithful, there will be blessings in my marriage (and then teach point number three above). At the end, remind children that God is watching. He sees all that we do in our relationships (and then teach point number four and number five above).

Discussion Questions

1. Do you plan to get married when you are older? Why or why not?
2. What lies does society tell you about marriage and purity? If a person believes and acts on any of these lies, according to Proverbs 5, what are the outcomes?
3. What is one important truth from Proverbs 5 that you think young people need to hear today? Why?

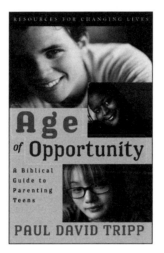

The argument over the last donut. The cry of nothing to wear a half hour before school. The "I'm the only one whose parents make them . . ."

Teenage hassles that disrupt parents' lives? Or prime opportunities to connect with, listen to, and nurture our kids?

Paul Tripp uncovers the heart issues affecting parents and their teenagers during the often chaotic adolescent years. With wit, wisdom, humility, and compassion, he shows parents how to seize the countless opportunities to deepen communication, learn, and grow with their teenagers.

"*Age of Opportunity* is a marvel. It brims with fresh, rich, honest truth."
    —David Powlison

"A wealth of biblical wisdom and a treasure of practical steps for understanding and shepherding your teen's heart."
    —Tedd Tripp

"Provides a superb road map for raising teenage children and experiencing with them the challenges, victories, and joys of our journey to maturity in Christ."
    —Ken Sande